S0-AFT-432

PENGUIN CLASSICS

ANTIGONE

SOPHOCLES was born at Colonus, just outside Athens, in 496 B.C. and lived ninety years. His long life spanned the rise and decline of the Athenian Empire, he was a friend of Pericles, and though not an active politician, he held several public offices, both military and civil. The leader of a literary circle and friend of Herodotus, Sophocles was interested in poetic theory as well as practice, and he wrote a prose treatise, *On the Chorus.* He seems to have been content to spend all his life at Athens and is said to have refused several invitations to royal courts. Sophocles first won a prize for tragic drama in 468, defeating the veteran Aeschylus. He wrote over a hundred plays for the Athenian theater and is said to have won the first prize at the City Dionysia eighteen times. Only seven of his tragedies are now extant. Fragments of other plays remain, showing that he drew on a wide range of themes; he also introduced the innovation of a third actor in his tragedies. He died in 406–5 B.C.

ROBERT FAGLES is Arthur W. Marks '19 Professor of Comparative Literature, Emeritus, at Princeton University. He is the recipient of the 1997 PEN/Ralph Manheim Medal for Translation and a 1996 Academy Award in Literature from the American Academy of Arts and Letters. Fagles has been elected to the Academy, the American Academy of Arts and Sciences, and the American Philosophical Society. He has translated the poems of Bacchylides. His translations of Sophocles' *Three Theban Plays,* Aeschylus' *Oresteia* (nominated for a National Book Award), and Homer's *Iliad* (winner of the 1991 Harold Morton Landon Translation Award by The Academy of American Poets, an award from the Translation Center of Columbia University, and the New Jersey Humanities Book Award) are published in Penguin Classics. His original poetry and his translations have appeared in many journals and reviews as well as in his book of poems, *I, Vincent: Poems from the Pictures of Van Gogh.* Mr. Fagles was one of the associate editors of Maynard Mack's Twickenham Edition of Alexander Pope's *Iliad* and *Odyssey,* and, with George Steiner, edited *Homer: A Collection of Critical Essays.* Mr. Fagles' most recent work is a translation of Homer's *Odyssey,* available from Penguin.

BERNARD KNOX is Director Emeritus of Harvard's Center for Hellenic Studies in Washington, D.C. His essays and reviews have appeared in numerous publications and in 1978 he won the George Jean Nathan Award for Dramatic Criticism. His works include *Oedipus at Thebes: Sophocles' Tragic Hero and His Time*; *The Heroic Temper: Studies in Sophoclean Tragedy*; *World and Action: Essays on the Ancient Theatre*; *Essays Ancient and Modern* (awarded the 1989 PEN/Spielvogel–Diamonstein Award); *The Oldest Dead White European Males and Other Reflections on the Classics*; and *Backing into the Future: The Classical Tradition and its Renewal*. He is the editor of *The Norton Book of Classical Literature* and has collaborated with Robert Fagles on the *Iliad* and the *Odyssey*.

SOPHOCLES
ANTIGONE

TRANSLATED BY
ROBERT FAGLES

INTRODUCTIONS AND
NOTES BY
BERNARD KNOX

PENGUIN BOOKS

PENGUIN BOOKS
Published by the Penguin Group
Penguin Books USA Inc.,
375 Hudson Street, New York, New York 10014, U.S.A.
Penguin Books Ltd, 80 Strand, London WC2R 0RL, England
Penguin Books Australia Ltd, 250 Camberwell Rd,
Camberwell, VIC 3124, Australia
Penguin Books Canada Ltd, 10 Alcorn Avenue,
Toronto, Ontario, Canada M4V 3B2
Penguin Books (N.Z.) Ltd, 182–190 Wairau Road,
Auckland 10, New Zealand

Penguin Books Ltd, Registered Offices:
Harmondsworth, Middlesex, England

First published in the United States of America by
Viking Penguin Inc. 1982
First published in Great Britain by Allen Lane 1982
Published in Penguin Classics 1984
Reprinted with revisions in 1984

ISBN 0 14 044.425 4
Library of Congress Catalog Card
Number 83-13053 (CIP data available)
Penguin Special Sales Edition ISBN: 0-14-243769-7
Printed in the United States of America

Set in Bembo

FOR KATYA, FOR NINA
tois philois d' orthôs philê

CONTENTS

ACKNOWLEDGMENTS   9

TRANSLATOR'S PREFACE   11

GREECE AND THE THEATER   13

INTRODUCTION TO ANTIGONE   33

ANTIGONE   55

NOTES ON THE TRANSLATION   127

ACKNOWLEDGMENTS

GRATEFUL acknowledgment is made to the following for permission to reprint copyrighted material.

Basic Books, Inc., and George Allen & Unwin: A selection from *The Interpretation of Dreams* by Sigmund Freud, translated and edited by James Strachey. Published in the United States by Basic Books, Inc., by arrangement with George Allen & Unwin and the Hogarth Press, Ltd.

New Directions Publishing Corp. and Faber and Faber Ltd: Two lines from "Ite" from *Personae* by Ezra Pound. Copyright 1926 by Ezra Pound.

University of Chicago Press: A selection from *The Iliad* by Homer, translated with an Introduction by Richmond Lattimore. Copyright 1951 by The University of Chicago.

The illustrations throughout the book were redrawn by Ann Gold from photographs of Mycenaean ornaments and seals from *Crete and Mycenae* by Spyridon Marinatos, published by Harry N. Abrams, Inc., New York, New York. The motif of the crown is from a gold funerary diadem for a woman, discovered in Schliemann's grave circle; the procession is from a gold signet ring from the lower town at Tiryns.

TRANSLATOR'S PREFACE

I HOPE the translation will speak for itself, but not before I say a word of thanks to many people for their help. First among them is Bernard Knox. In addition to writing the introductions and the notes, he determined the Greek text that we have used and tried to hold me closely to its meaning—tried, too, to make my English equal to the task. With countless comments on my work, as the work went through more versions than we can remember, he encouraged me to follow Pound's advice: "Seek ever to stand in the hard Sophoclean light / And take your wounds from it gladly."

Others have helped as well. Robert Fitzgerald spoke for himself and Dudley Fitts and generously left the gates of Thebes ajar. Francis Fergusson shared his conversation and his counsel. Several friends saw my drafts and offered me criticism or assent or a welcome blend of both: Nadia Benabid, Helen Bacon, Sandra Bermann, Toni Burbank, Rebecca Bushnell, Patricia Chappell, Robert Connor, Reginald Gibbons, Michael Goldman, Rachel Hadas, Katherine Hughes, Edmund Keeley, Nita Krevans, Jeffrey Perl, Richard Reid, Susan So, Theodore Weiss, Shira Wolosky and James Zetzel. Mrs. Robert Packer, my administrative aide, and Carol Szymanski lifted many burdens from my shoulders. Princeton University provided the leaves of absence that allowed me to finish the translation and, more important, the seminars in which I studied tragedy with my students.

From the outset, Alan Williams, my editor at The Viking Press, gave me his essential support. Elisabeth Sifton fortified my morale, Nanette Kritzalis, Anne Bass, Charles Verrill and Melissa Browne sped the production of the book, and many others— Juliet Annan, Nancy Gallt, Jean Griffin, Victoria Meyer and Constance Sayre—treated it with energy and warmth.

As the book appears in Penguin Classics now, my thanks

should go to several who are instrumental in the series. Betty Radice, the general editor, carefully read the play in manuscript and sent me her valuable suggestions. Kathryn Court, my editor and mainstay for the new edition, Marcia Burch, Dan Farley, Edward Iwanicki, Linda Rosenberg, Serena Kahn, and Neil Stuart—all were partisans of the translation in New York. With her fine style, Ann Gold designed *Antigone* to be a companion volume to my translation of Aeschylus' *Oresteia*. My English editor, Donald McFarlan, Peter Carson and Lorraine Cooper were gracious hosts at Allen Lane and Penguin Books in London.

Joined by Richard Simon, my agent Georges Borchardt used his skills and steady, heartening trust to find the book its home and help it on its way.

But the last word of thanks should go to Lynne—*tôi gar an kai meizoni / lexaim' an ê soi dia tychês toiasd' iôn?*

R.F.

Princeton, NJ.
1983

GREECE AND THE THEATER

IN THE sixth and fifth centuries before the birth of Christ an ancient civilization reached such heights of intellectual and artistic achievement that every succeeding period of Western culture, from the Roman Empire to the twentieth century, has been heavily in its debt, whether acknowledged or not. Those momentous years saw the beginnings of history and political theory (as well as political democracy) and the development of philosophical thought. In those years architects designed the temples which have dominated our concept of civic building ever since, and sculptors imposed on us an ideal vision of the human form which remains the point of reference even for those artists who turn against it. Not least among the achievements of this great age was the invention and perfection of an artistic medium which we take so unthinkingly for granted that we cannot imagine civilized life without it—the theater.

This outburst of creative energy in every field of endeavor took place in the eastern Mediterranean—Greece, the islands of the Aegean Sea and the Greek cities of the coast of Asia Minor. Earlier civilizations in this area—Babylon to the east and Egypt to the south, for example—had fertile river-valleys for an economic base, but Greece was (and still is) a poor country. "Greece and Poverty," said the historian Herodotus, "have always been bedfellows"; the land, as Odysseus says of Ithaca, his island home, is "a rugged place." From the air, as most travelers first see it now and as the vultures that circle over Apollo's shrine at Delphi always have, it is a forbidding sight. The bare mountain spines and ribs cross-hatch a disjointed grid from sea to sea, the armature of some gigantic statue that was never fleshed out. On the ground this first impression, modified in some details, holds good in the main: one entire third of the surface of Greece is naked rock on which nothing can grow or graze. The stark outlines of these mountains—peaks, range and valleys harshly clear from far away in the inexorable dry sunlight, softened only by the violet tone the twilight gives them for a few exquisite moments—these outlines are the frame and background of everything the Greeks saw. The mountains must have given them that sense of form, of the depth and solidity of natural shapes, which made them a race of sculptors and monumental builders, and it was in the mountains that they found the raw materials, limestone and marble, from which with chisel, hammer and drill they cut the stone images of their gods and columns for temples to house them. The mountains hemmed them in and cut them off from each other; as hard to cross in the winter snows as in the scorching heat of summer, they ringed the Greek horizon and made each lowland settlement a separate world.

Below the naked rock of the peaks, the trees, but there are not many left. Even in Plato's time, in the fourth century B.C., they were growing scarcer and, in fact, in his dialogue the *Critias* (the one which gave the world the myth of Atlantis) he has the Athenian aristocrat after whom the dialogue is named draw a nostalgic contrast between present and past. "What now remains compared with what existed then," he says, "is like the skeleton of a sick man, all the fat and soft earth wasted away and only the bare framework of the land left." He speaks longingly of a time when "the country was unspoiled: its mountains were arable highlands and what is now stony fields was once good soil. And the earth was enriched by the annual rains, which were not lost, as now, by flowing from the bare land into the sea . . . but the deep soil received and stored the water . . ." Since Plato's day things have got much worse; through the years the goats, the charcoalburners and the occupying armies have stripped most of the slopes. On those slopes, in the thickets of prickly shrub and among the rocks which burst into astonishing flower for a short spring season, roam the goats and, lower down, the sheep, herded by fierce dogs and fierce-looking shepherds. This is the no-man's-land of Greece, where unwanted children, like Oedipus, were left to die (but were saved by shepherds); where, not only in story but in grim reality, hunted men found refuge; where brigands and Klefts of the rebellions against the Turks, exiles and the Andartes of the Resistance and the Civil War, have all through Greece's bloody history escaped pursuit, reunited their scattered gangs and then descended like avenging furies on the plains below.

The plains are small, ringed by the mountains, or by mountains and sea, cut off from easy contact with one another; each one is a world apart, with, in ancient times, its own customs, dialect and separate government—the city-state. In the earlier civilizations of the Middle East the easy communications afforded by the rivers had made it possible, and the demands of irrigation, engineering and maintenance had made it necessary, to centralize control. These huge kingdoms, ruled from Babylon or Thebes, imposed uniform laws, taxes and worship over huge expanses of territory. But Greece was split up into separate small worlds: the plains, each with its own customs, laws, political institutions and traditions. They were such separate worlds that an ancient Greek joke book tells the story of a fool who saw the moon and asked his father: "Do they have a moon like that in other cities?"

These city-states were, as often as not, at war with their neighbors—over grazing land, borderlines or cattle raids. The Greeks, who gave us history, philosophy and political science, never managed to solve the problems posed by their political disunity; even the ideal states of their philosophers—the Republic of Plato, the perfect city of Aristotle—make provision for universal military training and active defense against external threats. This permanent insecurity in interstate relations reinforced the bond between citizen and citizen and at the same time directed their energies inward, to feed the competitive spirit that was so marked a feature of Greek life: competition in sports, in art, in politics.

Sometimes the competition was fiercer—for the means of subsistence, for life itself. The land of the plains, though fertile, never grew enough grain, the basic Greek staple, to feed a growing population. There was always a struggle between haves and have-nots; there were always men who had to leave home, either as exiles, to brood on their wrongs and plot for the day of return, or as colonists in search of a new site across the sea, to plow the land for grain and plant the other two basic crops, the olive and the vine. The olive trees, spaced out in regular patterns among the furrows, produced the rich green oil that was and still is an indispensable ingredient of every Greek dish. But the olive gave more than food; the inferior oil from the second or third pressings served as a sort of soap, rubbed into the pores and scraped off with a bronze tool, and as fuel for the small clay lamps which were the ancient Greek's only resource against the darkness. The vine, though the Greek variety seems a frail and puny plant compared with that of Burgundy, produced the wine without which no Greek could live content. Though they drank it sparingly— mixed one to three with water—it was essential to their communal and religious life.

Lowest and last, the sea. Almost tideless, it laps peacefully at the edges of the plains. It provided not only fish to supplement a diet in which meat was a rare luxury but also an easy way of communication with the outside world. Travel by land meant rough hill-tracks, and over those tracks heavy transport was difficult when not impossible; by sea, however, man and freight moved easily. When the Greek mercenaries of Xenophon's *Anabasis,* after months of marching and fighting in the mountains of Turkey, finally reached the Black Sea, one of them said, thankfully, "Now I can go home like Odysseus, flat on my back." And all around this inland sea, the Mediterranean, from Spain to Turkey—at Marseilles, Naples, Syracuse, to name only a few of their cities—the Greeks in search of a new home found everywhere the same climate, could grow the same crops. The sea was the true center of the Greek world: "we live round the sea," says Plato's Socrates, "like frogs . . . around a pond."

One of the frogs around the pond was the city of Athens, huddled beneath a rocky acropolis ten kilometers from the sea. It was the center of Greek intellectual and artistic life for most of the fifth century; it was also, for most of that time, the imperial ruler of the islands and coastal cities of the Aegean. In the early years of the century Athens had played a leading role in the defeat of an invading army from Persia, a huge empire which, based on what is now Iran, controlled the whole land mass from the Aegean coast to the border of India. When the Persian forces advanced south by land and sea against Athens, the inhabitants evacuated their city and took to their ships; the Persians burnt Athens, but the Athenian fleet (and its commander, Themistocles) played a major role in the decisive naval battle of Salamis (480 B.C.). A fifteen-year-old Sophocles, we are told, led the singers in the hymns of celebration and thanksgiving for the victory.

The Persian retreat from Europe was followed by a Greek counter-offensive, its aim the liberation of the Greeks of the islands and Asia Minor coasts. Sparta, the land power of the Greek alliance, withdrew from the enterprise, leaving Athens in effective command of the naval league against Persia. A series of stunning Athenian victories put an end to the Persian naval presence in the Aegean, but the newly liberated Greek cities soon found that they had merely exchanged one master for another. The contributions in ships and money, which had once been voluntary and intended for mutual defense, now became compulsory and were appropriated for Athenian use; cities that tried to leave the league were treated as rebels and subdued. The tribute money paid by the "allies" kept the Athenian fleet in being; it also helped defray the cost of the building program that, by the end of the century, made the Athenian acropolis one of the world's most famous architectural complexes. All this helped to provide employment for the Athenian people, whose well-being was not a matter to be neglected by their political leaders, since Athens was a democracy—by the end of the century a remarkably direct and radical democracy. The revenues of empire and profits from commercial operations promoted and protected by naval power also made possible that lavish expenditure on public festivals which Pericles, in his Funeral Speech, counted as one of the glories of Athenian democracy.

Among these festivals the most famous and popular was the Dionysia, the celebration of the god Dionysus, which took place

every spring, at the end of March or beginning of April. The
god was honored by performances, in the theater, of dithyrambs
(lyric hymns sung and danced by a chorus of fifty), tragedies and
comedies. Dionysus was a god whose territory was originally not
in the city at all. He was a god of the country but not of the level
plain that surrounds and feeds the city; he and his Maenads, ecstatic women who followed in his train, belonged to the wild—
on the vases where we see them painted they range through the
pine forests of the high slopes. The mythic accounts of his coming to Greece all tell the same story: his rites disrupted the normal pattern of city-state life, and the authorities acted against
him, only to be subdued by the god's irresistible power.

Whether or not these myths preserve some memory of actual
events we have no means of telling, but in fifth-century Athens
Dionysus was at home in the city; his statue was brought out
from the temple in the theater precinct to watch the plays. Seats
of honor were reserved for his priests (they are still there—
"Reserved for the priest of Dionysus" carved on the marble).
The four days of performance were a city festival, open to for-
eigners as well as citizens, a time when business was suspended,
when even prisoners were let out on bail so that they could
attend.

Dionysus is the life-spirit of all green vegetation—ivy, pine
tree and especially the vine; he is, in Dylan Thomas' phrase, "the
force that through the green fuse drives the flower." The drama
as we know it in the fifth century must have evolved or been
adapted from some kind of performance connected with his
worship. We do not know the details but there are some clear
connections. For one thing Dionysus is a popular rather than an
aristocratic religious figure, a late-comer to the Olympian pan-
theon immortalized in Homeric epic. His worship in Athens
seems to have been given official status under the anti-aristocratic
dictatorship of Pisistratus, the sixth-century prelude to the establishment of democracy, and the theater, his true ceremonial,
came to full growth under the democratic regime. For another,
Dionysus is often portrayed in contemporary vase painting as
masked or even as a mask; the actors in the theater played in

masks. And lastly Dionysus is a god whose worship can produce states of ecstatic possession, a loss of individual identity in the communal dance, and so perhaps may serve as a divine model for the actor's assumption of an alien personality as well as the audience's temporary identification with the masked figures onstage. In any case the important fact is not so much that the theater was the purlieu of a particular god as that it was from the beginning a sacramental area, a place where divine forces were invoked and put to work, where the performance was, for actors and audience alike, an act of worship.

The audience was, by our standards, immense; the theater building of the late fifth century, to judge from its ruins, could seat between fourteen and fifteen thousand spectators. They sat in rows that rise one above the other on the rocky southeastern slope of the Acropolis and border, for half of its circumference, a circular dancing floor behind which stood a wooden stage building. This was the actors' changing room, where they could change masks as well as costumes, to assume a different role; through its door (which for the audience was the door of the royal palace of Thebes or, with scenic modifications, the entry to the wood of the Erinyes) the actors made their exits and their entrances, though they could also go behind the stage building and approach the acting area from the side, as visitors from the city or abroad. The masks (which made it possible for the male actors to play female parts as well as to play more than one character) were not the grotesque caricatures we know from modern theater decorations; contemporary vase paintings show that they were naturalistic representations of types—bearded king, old man, young girl and so on. The play of facial expression we expect from our actors was in any case ruled out in an open-air theater where the top row of spectators was over fifty-five yards away from the stage area; individuality of character had to be created by the poet's word and the actor's delivery and gesture. By the end of the century the parts were played by professional actors, three for each tragedy, assigned to the dramatists by the magistrate in charge of the festival. Aeschylus, the first great dramatist (who had fought in the ships at Salamis), acted in his own plays; Sophocles followed his example but then, we are told, abandoned the stage because his voice was not strong enough. His younger contemporary and competitor, Euripides (born in the year Salamis was fought) never, as far as we know, appeared on stage.

In addition to actors and spectators, there was a third element of the performance, one older than either of these two. It was the chorus—a Greek word that means "dance"; the chorus of Greek tragedies sang, but it was also and had been in origin a group of dancers. The way Greek theaters are built shows how central to the performance the chorus was; the rows of stone benches one below the other all the way down the hillside focus the spectators' vision not on the stage area but on the circular dancing floor. Choral performances in Greece are much older than the drama; from time immemorial dancers had worshiped the gods, celebrated athletic (and military) victories, mourned the dead and danced on the circular threshing floors which are still to be found on Greek hillsides and which are probably the original of the circular dancing floor in the theater. Drama as we know it was created when an Athenian named Thespis added to the dance and song of the chorus the speech of an actor. With the addition of a second actor, the performers could develop from a sort of dramatic narrative—actor to chorus—to a dramatic relationship—actor to actor—or even a dramatic conflict—actor against actor. This second actor was introduced by Aeschylus, and it is this innovation that entitles him to be called, as he often has been, the creator of tragedy. When Sophocles later added a third actor, the complicated play of relationships between the actors came to dominate the scene, reducing the role of the chorus to that of commentator, where before it had been active participant. But the chorus was always there, and it has an important function: it is an emotional bridge between spectators and actors. An anonymous crowd with only a group identity—Theban citizens, inhabitants of Colonus or whatever—it functioned on stage as if the audience itself were part of the action; all the more so because, unlike the professional actors, the chorus consisted of citizen amateurs, representing their tribal group in the dramatic competition.

For, like almost all Greek institutions, the festival of Dionysus was a contest. Three dramatists on three successive days presented their plays and at the end were awarded first, second or third prize. What these prizes were we do not know; they may have been monetary but they cannot have been substantial enough for anyone to expect to make a living by producing plays. (Sophocles' father seems to have been the wealthy owner of some kind of factory, and his son was educated by the most famous teachers of the day.) The real reward of a first prize was the glory and the admiration of one's fellow-citizens; Sophocles had his full share of such rewards, for we have evidence that he won the first prize at the Dionysia eighteen times, and it is recorded that he never won the third prize. The glory of a first prize was shared by the poet with the chorus, the actors and the *chorêgos,* a private citizen who had paid out of his own pocket for the rich costumes, the training of the chorus and a host of other expenses. He was not, however, as he would be today, the "producer," an entrepreneur who puts the package together for profit. In fact he was a rich citizen, designated by the city authorities for this function; his part in the proceedings was, in effect, a form of enlightened taxation.

The theater was not only a religious festival, it was also an aspect of the city's political life. Athens in the fifth century was a democracy, an increasingly inclusive and participatory one as the century advanced. This radically democratic system was reflected in the organization of the dramatic festival. The prizes were awarded at the end by ten judges, elected on the opening day by lot and sworn to impartiality. Feelings often ran high, and these judges must have been under considerable pressure from the audience. In 468 B.C., the year in which Sophocles first entered the contest, competing against Aeschylus, the tension was such that the magistrate appointed as judges the ten elected generals for that year, among them Cimon, the hero of the naval crusade against Persia. (They gave Sophocles the first prize.) The whole festival reflected not only the organization but also the pride and achievement of the city of Athens. When, later in the century, the league against Persia had become an Athenian maritime empire, the tribute money of the subject cities was brought to

Athens at the time of the dramatic festival and displayed in the theater before the plays were performed. The orphaned children of those Athenians who had fallen in battle were cared for and educated by the city; once they had reached young manhood, they were paraded in the theater in full armor, to receive the blessings of the people. Honors and distinctions decreed for foreign heads of state and individuals were conferred in the theater at the festival.

The dramatist who composed and produced the new plays for such an occasion was in a situation unique in the history of the theater. An audience of some fourteen thousand citizens, conscious of the religious solemnity of the occasion and the glory it reflected on the city and the individuals responsible, packed the benches of the theater to hear, as the sun rose, the first lines of the play. A modern reader might expect that a theater such as this would produce drama that was, to use a cant phrase, "relevant, living theater," based on contemporary themes, current issues. At the end of a day's performance in Athens, when the comic poet came on stage, the audience did in fact enjoy a ribald, frank, hard-hitting treatment of contemporary themes—with no holds barred—in which prominent statesmen and individual citizens were held up to ridicule in a style that few modern states would permit. But the first three plays of the day's performance were tragedy, and here, with very few exceptions, the figures who walked the stage, far from being contemporary, were men, women and gods from the far-off past, from the dim beginnings of the youth of the race—an age of heroes and heroines, the legends of the beginnings of the Greek world. The stuff from which the tragic poet made his plays was not contemporary reality but myth. And yet it did reflect contemporary reality, did so perhaps in terms more authoritative because they were not colored by the partisan emotions of the time, terms which were in fact so authoritative that they remain meaningful even for us today.

This is not as paradoxical as it sounds. The dramatist who had one of his characters define the role of the theater as "to hold . . . the mirror up to nature, to show . . . the very age and body of the time his form and pressure," and the actors as "the abstract and brief chronicles of the time," did not set even one of his plays in the Elizabethan England he lived in; his scenes are set in the far past—ancient Rome, medieval England—or in far-off places—Illyria, Bohemia or that magic island of *The Tempest*. Shakespeare used for his plots printed sources—Italian novels, English chronicles, translations of ancient biographies—but the sources of the Greek dramatists were, for the most part, oral; they were the myths, the stories that were told about the past and which, since everyone told the stories differently, offered infinite variety to the playwright.

But this material offered more than variety of dramatic incident. These myths were the only national memory of the remote past, of a time before the Greeks invented the alphabet, so that, shifting and changing though they might be, they had the authority, for the audience, of what we call history. The masked actors on stage were the great figures of the audience's past, their ancestors. Since the myths, retold from generation to generation, were shaped by the selective emphasis of an oral tradition that preserved and created images of universal significance, the masked actors presented to the audience not only historical figures from their past but also poetic symbols of their life and death, their ambitions, fears and hopes. But the myths also had the authority of religion; these stories are the sacred tales of religious cult and recall (or rather create) a time when men and gods were closer than they have been ever since. It so happens that in the play presented here the gods do not appear on stage (though they do in other Sophoclean tragedies), but the audience is never allowed to forget them. The characters of the play appeal to them constantly, and the action raises questions about their role: *Antigone* explores the mystery of the divine purposes. The masked actors offered the audience not only a vision of its past, not only great historic figures molded by the oral tradition into shapes symbolic of all human hopes and fears, but also, invoked at every turn if not actually present on stage, those gods whose dispensation of good and evil to mankind seemed to pass all understanding.

Though the details of these traditional stories varied considerably from one teller of the tale to another (and especially from one city to another), and though the dramatist could (and often did) invent new variations, the main outlines of the best-known stories were fairly stable—Oedipus always kills his father and marries his mother, Eteocles and Polynices must kill each other. The dramatist who used this material derived a double benefit from the audience's knowledge of the stories: he could either lull them into expecting the familiar—and so increase the shock effect of some radical innovation in the story—or, renouncing surprise, he could pose the ignorant pronouncements of his characters against the audience's knowledge of their future and so produce dramatic irony. Sophocles was a master of this technique, and *Oedipus the King* the supreme example of its effective use; almost every statement made by Oedipus has a second, sinister meaning for the audience, which knows, as he does not, his past and his future. These grim reverberations are especially powerful in tragedies concerned, as this play is from start to finish, with destiny, divine dispensation and the human situation. The audience, with its knowledge of the past and the future, is on the level of the gods; they see the ambition, passion and actions of the characters against the larger pattern of their lives and deaths. The spectator is involved emotionally in the heroic struggles of the protagonist, a man like himself, and at the same time can view his heroic action from the standpoint of superior knowledge, the knowledge possessed by those gods whose prophecies of the future play so large a role in Sophoclean tragedy. This play gave its audience an image of human life as they saw and lived it, precarious and unpredictable, but also as it must appear to the all-seeing eye of divine omniscience.

The Athenian dramatists found this age-old and powerful material ready to hand; what they did was to add another dimension to it. The stories came from a time when the city was not the full context of men's lives; the myths recall the days of migrations, of the chaotic years of conquest and eventual settlement—a time when great heroic individuals imposed their wills, when tribal, family relationships were infinitely stronger than the bond between citizens, a time in fact before the city made its laws and established its primacy. But the Attic tragedians, in play after play, set these heroes, in their actions and suffering, against the background of the city. The ancient myths (and the epic tradition that first gave them literary form) were concerned with the fate of the hero; the drama is concerned also with the fate of the city which he defends, attacks, rules or represents. And the chorus, which is a representation on stage of the community, constantly calls attention by its very presence as well as its song to this larger dimension.

The fifth-century Athenian prided himself on the fact that he was a fully responsible and active citizen; "each individual," said Pericles in his panegyric of Athenian democracy, the Funeral Speech, "is interested not only in his own affairs but in the affairs of the city as well . . . we Athenians in our own persons take our decisions on policy or submit them to proper discussion." Sophocles was no exception; in fact he was deeply involved in public affairs throughout his long career. He served, for example, as one of the treasurers of the league against Persia in 443 B.C. and as one of the ten generals in command of the fleet charged with suppressing the revolt of Samos some years later. These were the years of Athens' unchallenged greatness; under the leadership of Pericles she steadily built up her influence abroad as well as her economic resources at home. In 431 B.C. those cities of the Peloponnese which had been Athens' allies against Persia, alarmed by the dynamic growth of Athens' power and evident ambition to become the dominant Greek state, provoked a war that lasted twenty-seven years and ended in Athenian defeat.

Pericles died in the third year of this war, but Sophocles lived on almost to the end. In 411 B.C., after Athens suffered a catastrophic defeat in Sicily (the end of a megalomaniac attempt to conquer that rich but distant island), Sophocles was called in to serve on a special board of commissioners to deal with the political and military crisis. In 406 B.C., as the news reached Athens that Euripides had died in Macedonia, Sophocles brought on his chorus dressed in mourning as a tribute to his younger rival. A few months later he himself died at the age of ninety. In the winter after his death the comic poet Aristophanes paid a light-hearted compliment to the memory not so much of the poet as of the man the Athenians mourned and had loved. In his play *The Frogs* the god Dionysus, disgusted with the pitiful productions of the younger dramatists, goes down to Hades to bring Euripides back to life. Asked why he doesn't bring Sophocles instead, he says first that he wants to see how Iophon, Sophocles' son and fellow-tragedian, will do without his father's help, and then adds: "Besides, Euripides, who is a scoundrel, will be more than ready to break out and run off with me. But Sophocles was an easy-going man up here—and will be down there too."

This estimate fits perfectly into the only detailed account of him we have from the pen of a contemporary. Ion of Chios, himself a tragic poet, gives us a specimen of Sophocles' brilliant literary conversation at a banquet held in his honor as he was on his way to Samos to serve as a general under Pericles. He also describes the skillful maneuver that enabled the poet to snatch a kiss from the handsome boy who was serving the wine. As the company applauded, Sophocles said: "I am practicing strategy, gentlemen—since Pericles says that I know how to make poems but not how to be a general. Don't you think my stratagem was successful?" Ion adds that this was typical "of his wit in word and action when the wine was served. But in public life," he goes on, "his conduct was not that of an expert or an activist, it was like that of any well-bred Athenian." One other contemporary source gives the same impression of this remarkable personality, whose long, successful life and universal popularity seem an unlikely source for the tragic world he created on the Attic stage. Phrynichus, another comic poet, wrote an epitaph for him (almost certainly in the play that competed with Aristophanes' *Frogs*): "Blessed Sophocles, who lived a long life, a happy man and a clever one. He composed many fine tragedies and died well, without enduring any misfortune." One great misfortune he escaped by his death: he did not live to see his beloved Athens starved into surrender in 405–4 B.C., the Spartan fleet in the Piraeus, the Long Walls demolished, the end of Athens' great age.

Of the 123 plays our ancient sources credit him with, only

seven have survived intact. Three of them, *Antigone, Oedipus the King* and *Oedipus at Colonus,* are based on the saga of Thebes, the city of seven gates. We do not know the precise dates for the production of these three plays, but our meager evidence suggests that *Antigone* came first (perhaps in 442 B.C.), *Oedipus the King* next (some time soon after 430 B.C.), and *Oedipus at Colonus* last (in fact it was produced after Sophocles' death).

This does not correspond to the order of the mythical events in the Theban saga. The story was told in many different ways; Sophocles' version (some of it is undoubtedly his own invention) ran roughly as follows. Laius and Jocasta, king and queen of Thebes, told by Apollo at Delphi that any son they had would kill its father, sent their infant out, its feet pierced with metal pins, to die on the mountainside. But the shepherd who was supposed to abandon it gave it instead to a fellow-shepherd, who came from the other side of Cithaeron, the mountain range between Thebes and Corinth. This shepherd took the child to Polybus and Merope, king and queen of Corinth; they adopted it, for they were childless. They named the child Oedipus (the name suggests, in Greek, "swell-foot"). When he was a grown man, a drunken guest told him that he was not the true son of the royal house; his foster-parents tried to reassure him, but he went to Delphi to ask Apollo. There he was told he would kill his father and marry his mother. He resolved never to return to Corinth; instead of going home, southeast by boat, he went east on foot through the defiles of Mount Parnassus and, at a narrow place where three roads met, quarreled over the right of way with an old man in a wagon. Attacked, he defended himself, killing the old man and (so he thought) all his retainers. The old man was his father, Laius.

Oedipus came down to the plain where the citizens of Thebes were oppressed by a monster, the Sphinx a winged lion with a human, female face. She would leave them alone only when she got an answer to her riddle; many had tried to guess it, failed and been killed. The Thebans promised a great reward to anyone who could free them from the Sphinx: the throne of Thebes and the hand of Jocasta, the widowed queen. Oedipus answered the riddle. "What is it that goes on four feet, three feet and two feet . . . and is most feeble when it walks on four?" His answer was "man—on all fours as a baby, on two feet at maturity, on three as an old man with a stick." The Sphinx threw herself to death off the rocks, and Oedipus entered the city to claim his reward.

For many years he was the successful and beloved ruler of Thebes; he was also the father of two sons, Eteocles and Polynices, and two daughters, Antigone and Ismene. Suddenly a plague struck the city, and the Delphic oracle declared it would cease only when the murderer of Laius was found, to be exiled or executed. Oedipus, after pronouncing a solemn curse on the unknown murderer, proceeded, by persistent questioning and stubborn pursuit of the investigation, to find him. In the process he also discovered his own true identity and recognized that the prophecy made to him long ago at Delphi had been fulfilled. Jocasta hanged herself, and Oedipus, taking the long pins from her robe, put out his eyes. Creon, Jocasta's brother, assumed power in Thebes, ruling together with the two sons of Oedipus. They offended their father and, after pronouncing a curse on them (that they should die by each other's hand), he left Thebes, with Antigone as his guide, to become a wandering beggar on the highways of Greece.

At Thebes the two sons of Oedipus quarreled over their right to the throne; Eteocles prevailed and Polynices left to find allies abroad. At Argos he raised an army, led by seven champions (the Seven against Thebes). Meanwhile the Delphic oracle announced that Oedipus' grave would be the site of victory for the city in whose territory it lay: the blind beggar became a prize to be won. While Creon, acting for Eteocles, and Polynices, acting on his own behalf, set out to find him, the old man had arrived at the hamlet of Colonus just outside Athens. Learning that the wood where he had taken shelter was sacred to the Eumenides, he realized that he had come to his last resting place. Apollo had prophesied this years ago and also told him that by his choice of burial place he could reward his friends and punish his enemies. He decided to confer this gift of victory on Athens, which, in the person of Theseus its king, welcomed him generously and made him a citizen. Attempts to win him for Thebes by Creon and by Polynices for Argos met with failure; Oedipus, summoned by the gods, went to a mysterious death at Colonus, to become a protector, in his grave, of Athenian soil.

Polynices went back to Argos and led his troops against Thebes; the attack was beaten off, and Oedipus' prophetic curse was fulfilled—brother killed brother. Creon, now sole ruler, denied burial to the corpse of Polynices; the penalty for disobedience to this decree was death. It was defied by Antigone, who, captured and brought before Creon, defended her action so resolutely and uncompromisingly that he ordered her imprisoned in an underground tomb, where she would starve to death. He rejected the plea of his son Haemon, who was betrothed to her, and the warning of the prophet Tiresias, who told him that his refusal of burial to the corpse offended the gods. But second thoughts prevailed; he buried Polynices and went to release Antigone. He came too late; she had hanged herself, and Haemon, who had found her body, killed himself in her tomb. Creon's wife, hearing the news, killed herself, cursing her husband for the loss of her son. Creon was left alone to face a second attack on Thebes, a successful one this time, by the *Epigonoi*, the sons of the seven champions who had fallen at the seven gates.

The three Sophoclean plays, arranged according to their place in the saga, would produce the sequence *Oedipus the King, Oedipus at Colonus, Antigone,* and the plays are usually, in translation, presented in that order. Such a sequence however misleads unwary readers into thinking of the plays as a "trilogy" (or a "cycle")—a dramatic unit like the three plays of the *Oresteia* of Aeschylus or of O'Neill's *Mourning Becomes Electra.* Though there are many indications in the texts that Sophocles in the final Oedipus play had the earlier one firmly in mind, each play is a completely independent unit and in fact, though a character may appear in all three (Creon, for example), the point of view from which he is seen differs from one play to another. And in all three plays the mythical antecedents are slightly different; in *Antigone,* to cite just one instance, the heroine refers to the death of Oedipus in terms ("hated, / his reputation in ruins," lines 61–62 of the translation) that are incompatible with *Oedipus at Colonus.* It seems best therefore to read the three plays as Sophocles wrote them and the Athenian audience saw them: *Antigone* first, before the outbreak of the disastrous war; *Oedipus the King* next, during the early years of the war and after the Athenian plague of 429 B.C.; and lastly *Oedipus at Colonus,* an old man's play about an old man, written in the desperate final days of the war and produced in 401 B.C. after the poet's death.

But there is also a positive reason for reading the plays in chronological order: they represent successive stages in Sophocles' development as a dramatist and tragic poet. This is not a development that can be plotted in detail; we have only a pitiful remnant of his life's work—seven plays out of 123—and attempts to assess such changes in dramatic method as well as intellectual content are notoriously subjective. Nevertheless it seems safe to say that *Oedipus at Colonus,* written in the poet's last years, expresses a different tragic vision from that which lies behind *Antigone,* written over thirty years earlier, and that *Oedipus the King,* though it deals with themes common to all three plays, is still another modification of the basic tragic view. The plays read in their order of composition suggest a changing concept of the fundamental problems posed in Sophoclean tragedy; those problems and the poet's attitude toward them are the focus of the introductory essay that follows.

ANTIGONE

INTRODUCTION

THIS PLAY, it is generally agreed, was produced before and fairly close to the year 441 B.C. Sophocles, as we know from a reliable contemporary source, was one of the nine generals elected, with Pericles, for a campaign against the revolt of Samos in that year. The ancient introduction to the play, found in most of the manuscripts, records a tradition that Sophocles owed his election to office to the popularity of *Antigone*. True or false, this story could only have been based on a widely accepted belief that the play was produced before the year 441.

The story also, by setting *Antigone* in a political context, draws attention to the political content of the play, its concern with the problems of the *polis,* the city-state. *Antigone* resurfaces in a highly political context once again in the fourth century, some sixty years after Sophocles' death; it had by that time become a classic. The orator and statesman Demosthenes had the clerk of the court read out Creon's speech on the proper loyalties of a citizen (lines 194–214 of the translation) as a lesson in patriotism to his political opponent Aeschines (who had once been a professional actor and had played the part of Creon). And in that same century Aristotle quoted the play repeatedly in his treatise the *Politics.*

To the modern world, particularly the world of Victorian England, with its comfortable belief in progress and its confidence that such barbaric acts as exposure of an enemy's corpse were a thing of a distant past, the subject matter of the play seemed academic. Matthew Arnold wrote in 1853 that it was "no longer possible that we should feel a deep interest in the *Antigone* of Sophocles." The twentieth century has lost any such illusions. Two modern adaptations of the play, both of them alive with political urgency, are highlights in the history of the modern theater. In February 1944, in a Paris occupied by the German army, four months before the Allied landings in Normandy, Jean Anouilh produced his *Antigone,* a play in which Antigone is unmistakably identified with the French resistance movement. This is clear from the frequent threats of torture leveled at the heroine (not to be found in Sophocles but characteristic of Gestapo interrogations); the fact, well known to everyone in the audience, that the German Nazi military police often exposed the corpses of executed resistance fighters as a deterrent; and finally from the brilliant characterization of Creon's guards, whose low social origins, vulgar language and callous brutality accurately recall the contemporary *miliciéns,* the French fascist terror squads, which were more feared and hated than the Gestapo itself. The reason the German authorities allowed the production of the play is its treatment of Creon. Anouilh presents him as a practical man whose assumption of power faces him with a tragic dilemma: his desire to rule firmly but fairly, to restore and maintain order in a chaotic situation, is frustrated by a determined, fanatical, apparently irrational resistance. These are exactly the terms in which the German military authorities would have described their own position in occupied France. At the first performance the play was greeted with applause from both the French and Germans in the audience.

The other modern adaptation, Bertolt Brecht's radical revision of Hölderlin's translation, staged at Chur in Switzerland in 1948, was less ambivalent. The prologue is a scene in a Berlin air-raid shelter, March 1945, and it is all too clear what Creon is meant to suggest to the audience: he has launched Thebes on an aggressive war against Argos, and Polynices (conscripted by Creon in Brecht's violent reworking of the legend) has been killed for deserting the battle line when he saw his brother Eteocles fall. At the end of the play the tide turns against Thebes as Argos counterattacks; Creon takes Thebes down with him to destruction rather than surrender. Against this Hitlerian black, Antigone is all white; she is the image of what Brecht longed to see—the rising of the German people against Hitler, a resistance that in fact never came to birth. The poem Brecht wrote for the program of the production, an address to Antigone—

Come out of the twilight
and walk before us a while,
friendly, with the light step
of one whose mind is fully made up . . .

—reminds us that Brecht was a lyric poet as well as a dramatist,
but it is a dream poem, a lament, a regret for that rising of a
whole people against fascism, which Brecht's political creed ur-
gently demanded but which never came "out of the twilight."

Of these two modern adaptations, Anouilh's, which presents
the conflict between the protagonists as a real dilemma, is closer
to the spirit of the Sophoclean play than Brecht's passionate ad-
vocacy of one side against the other. For in the opening scenes of
the Sophoclean play Creon is presented in a light that the
original audience was certain to regard as favorable: he is the
defender of the city, the eloquent champion of its overriding
claim on the loyalty of its citizens in time of danger. His opening speech, a declaration of principles, contains echoes of Pericles' Funeral Speech; since that speech was delivered in the winter
of 431–30 B.C., long after the first performance of *Antigone,* it
seems likely that these phrases come from the common stock of
democratic patriotic oratory. The particular action that Creon
tries to justify by this general appeal, the exposure of Polynices'
corpse, may have caused the audience some uneasiness, but on
his main point, that loyalty to the city takes precedence over
any private loyalty, to friend or family, they would have agreed
with him.

As the chorus obviously does. They express sympathy for
Antigone only in the scene where she is led off to her death, and
even then in such grudging terms that she takes their declaration
as derision. Only when they hear from Tiresias the verdict of the
gods and realize from his prophecy of wars to come that Creon's
action threatens the city with disaster, do they advise him to
countermand his edict. For them the interests of the city are
paramount. In the magnificent ode that they sing after the sentry
comes to tell Creon that his orders have already been defied, they
celebrate the progress of the human race from savagery to civi-

lization: its culmination is the creation of the city. Man has become master of the sea and land, caught the birds of the air and tamed the beasts of the wild and taught himself speech and "the mood and mind for law that rules the city" (396). They end the song with a caution that man's ingenuity and resourcefulness may lead him to disaster unless he "weaves in / the laws of the land, and the justice of the gods" and they repudiate the man of "reckless daring" (409–10, 415). By the end of the play the audience, if they remember these words, will think of Creon, but at this point the chorus is clearly thinking of the unidentified rebel who has defied the city's ruler and thrown a symbolic handful of dust on the corpse of the city's bitter enemy who was once her friend. They accept, as most of the audience did, Creon's manifesto: "our country *is* our safety. / Only while she voyages true on course / can we establish friendships . . ." (211–13).

This is not to say that Creon is right to order the exposure of the corpse; in fact, by the end of the play it is made clear that his action is a violation of divine law, and besides he has by then long since abandoned any claim to speak for the citizen body as a whole and in their best interest. "Am I to rule this land for others—or myself?" (823) he asks his son Haemon. There is no doubt about what he thinks is the correct answer to that question. But before he is driven by the consequences of Antigone's defiance to reveal his true and deepest motives, he represents a viewpoint few Greeks would have challenged: that in times of crisis, the supreme loyalty of the citizen is to the state and its duly constituted authorities.

It is important to remember this since the natural instinct of all modern readers and playgoers is to sympathize fully with Antigone, the rebel and martyr. This is of course a correct instinct; in the end the gods, through their spokesman, the prophet Tiresias, uphold her claim that divine law does indeed prescribe burial for all dead men. But though she appeals to this law—"the great unwritten, unshakable traditions" (505)—in her magnificent challenge to Creon, she has other motives too. She proclaims again and again, to her sister Ismene as to her opponent Creon, the duty she owes to her brother, to the family relation-

ship. "If I had allowed / my own mother's son to rot, an unburied corpse"—she tells the king, "that would have been an
agony!" (520–22). "He is my brother," she tells her sister Ismene,
"and—deny it as you will— / your brother too" (55–56). Creon's
denial of burial to the corpse of Polynices has assaulted this fierce
devotion to blood relationship at a particularly sensitive point,
for the funeral rites, especially the emotional lament over the
dead, were, in an ancient Greek household, the duty and privi-
lege of the women. (In the villages of Greece today they still are.)
Antigone and Ismene are the last surviving women of the house
of Oedipus; this is why it seems to Antigone that Creon's decree
is aimed particularly at them—"the martial law our good Creon /
lays down for you and me" (37–38)—and why she takes it for
granted Ismene will help her and turns so contemptuously and
harshly against her when she refuses.

Antigone's dedicated loyalty to the family is, however, more
than a private code of conduct; in the context of fifth-century
Athens her challenge to the authority of the city-state and defense of a blood relationship had strong political overtones.
Athenian democratic institutions were egalitarian beyond anything conceivable in modern societies (many important magis-
tracies, for example, were filled by lot, not election), but Athens
had for centuries before the establishment of democracy been
ruled by the great aristocratic families that traced their descent
from heroic or divine ancestors, and these families were still, under the democracy, powerful, cohesive, exclusive groups, which
maintained their separate identities through religious cults and
family priesthoods. They were powerful concentrations of pa-
tronage and influence, and they worked, within the democratic
institutions, openly or through unseen connections, for the ad-
vancement and interests of their members (a phenomenon not
unknown in modern Greece as well).

The political aspect of Antigone's loyalty is emphasized at once
in Creon's inaugural address: "whoever places a friend [the Greek
word *philos* also means "relative"] / above the good of his own
country, he is nothing" (203–4). And when he realizes later that
this is in fact the issue between him and his niece, he reconfirms

her death sentence with a sarcastic reference to Zeus *Homaimos,* the divinity especially associated with the family worship: "let her cry for mercy, sing her hymns / to Zeus who defends all bonds of kindred blood" (735–36).

Antigone appeals not only to the bond of kindred blood but also to the unwritten law, sanctioned by the gods, that the dead must be given proper burial—a religious principle. But Creon's position is not anti-religious; in fact he believes that he has religion on his side. The gods, for him, are the gods of the city, which contains and protects their shrines, celebrates their festivals and sacrifices, and prays to them for deliverance; Creon finds it unthinkable that these gods should demand the burial of a traitor to the city who came with a foreign army at his back

> to burn their temples ringed with pillars,
> . . . scorch their hallowed earth
> and fling their laws to the winds.   (323–25)

Once again, there would have been many in the audience who felt the same way. These vivid phrases would have recalled to them the destruction of Athens and the desecration of its temples by the Persian invaders in 480; they would have had no second thoughts about denying burial to the corpse of any Athenian who had fought on the Persian side. Denial of burial in their homeland to traitors, real or supposed, was not unknown in Greece. Themistocles, for example, the hero of the Persian War, was later driven from Athens by his political enemies, who accused him of pro-Persian conspiratorial activity. Hounded from one Greek city to another he finally took refuge in Persian-controlled territory, where he died. When his relatives wished to bring his bones back to be buried in Athenian soil, permission was refused. Creon's decree of course goes much further and forbids burial altogether, but the Athenian attitude toward Themistocles shows that for Sophocles' audience the decree did not sound as outlandishly barbaric as it does to us. In the play, the opening song of the chorus gives tense expression to the terror inspired in the Theban people by Polynices' treacherous attack, their hatred of the foreign warlords he has marshaled against them, and their joy at their own deliverance and his defeat and death.

The opening scenes show us the conflicting claims and loyalties of the two adversaries, solidly based, in both cases, on opposed political and religious principles. This is of course the basic insight of Hegel's famous analysis of the play: he sees it as "a collision between the two highest moral powers." What is wrong with them, in his view, is that they are both "one-sided." But Hegel goes much further than that. He was writing in the first half of the nineteenth century, a period of fervent German nationalism in which the foundations of the unified German state were laid: his views on loyalty to the state were very much those of Creon. "Creon," he says, "is not a tyrant, he is really a moral power. He is not in the wrong."

However, as the action develops the favorable impression created by Creon's opening speech is quickly dissipated. His announcement of his decision to expose the corpse, the concluding section of his speech, is couched in violent, vindictive terms—"carrion for the birds and dogs to tear" (230)—which stand in shocking contrast to the ethical generalities that precede it. This hint of a cruel disposition underlying the statesmanlike façade is broadened by the threat of torture leveled at the sentry (344–50) and the order to execute Antigone in the presence of Haemon, her betrothed (852–54). And as he meets resistance from a series of opponents—Antigone's contemptuous defiance, the rational, political advice of his son Haemon, the imperious summons to obedience of the gods' spokesman, Tiresias—he swiftly abandons the temperate rhetoric of his inaugural address for increasingly savage invective. Against the two sanctions invoked by Antigone, the demands of blood relationship, the rights and privileges of the gods below, he rages in terms ranging from near-blasphemous defiance to scornful mockery.

> Sister's child or closer in blood
> than all my family clustered at my altar
> worshiping Guardian Zeus—she'll never escape,
> . . . the most barbaric death.
>
> (543–46)

He will live to regret this wholesale denial of the family bond, for it is precisely through that family clustered at his altar that his punishment will be administered, in the suicides of his son and his wife, both of whom die cursing him.

And for Antigone's appeals to Hades, the great god of the underworld to whom the dead belong, Creon has nothing but contempt; for him "Hades" is simply a word meaning "death," a sentence he is prepared to pass on anyone who stands in his way. He threatens the sentry with torture as a prelude: "simple death won't be enough for you" (348). When asked if he really intends to deprive Haemon of his bride he answers sarcastically: "Death will do it for me" (648). He expects to see Antigone and Ismene turn coward "once they see Death coming for their lives" (655). With a derisive comment he tells his son to abandon Antigone: "Spit her out, / . . . Let her find a husband down among the dead [in Hades' house]" (728–30). And he dismisses Antigone's reverence for Hades and the rights of the dead with mockery as he condemns her to be buried alive: "There let her pray to the one god she worships: / Death" (875–76). But this Hades is not something to be so lightly referred to, used or mocked. In the great choral ode which celebrated Man's progress and powers this was the one insurmountable obstacle that confronted him:

> ready, resourceful man!
>   Never without resources
> never an impasse as he marches on the future—
> only Death, from Death alone he will find no rescue . . .   (401–4)

And Creon, in the end, looking at the corpse of his son and hearing the news of his wife's suicide, speaks of Hades for the first time with the fearful respect that is his due, not as an instrument of policy or a subject for sardonic word-play, but as a divine power, a dreadful presence: "harbor of Death, so choked, so hard to cleanse!— / why me? why are you killing me?" (1413–14).

Creon is forced at last to recognize the strength of those social and religious imperatives that Antigone obeys, but long before this happens he has abandoned the principles which he had proclaimed as authority for his own actions. His claim to be representative of the whole community is forgotten as he refuses to accept Haemon's report that the citizens, though they dare not speak out, disapprove of his action; he denies the relevance of such a report even if true—"And is Thebes about to tell me how to rule?" (821)—and finally repudiates his principles in specific terms by an assertion that the city belongs to him—"The city *is* the king's—that's the law!" (825). This autocratic phrase puts the finishing touch to the picture Sophocles is drawing for his audience: Creon has now displayed all the characteristics of the "tyrant," a despotic ruler who seizes power and retains it by intimidation and force. Athens had lived under the rule of a "tyrant" before the democracy was established in 508 B.C., and the name and institution were still regarded with abhorrence. Creon goes on to abandon the gods whose temples crown the city's high places, the gods he once claimed as his own, and his language is even more violent. The blind prophet Tiresias tells him that the birds and dogs are fouling the altars of the city's gods with the carrion flesh of Polynices; he must bury the corpse. His furious reply begins with a characteristic accusation that the prophet has been bribed (the sentry had this same accusation flung at him), but what follows is a hideously blasphemous defiance of those gods Creon once claimed to serve:

> You'll never bury that body in the grave,
> not even if Zeus's eagles rip the corpse
> and wing their rotten pickings off to the throne of god! (1151–53)

At this high point in his stubborn rage (he will break by the end of the scene and try, too late, to avoid the divine wrath), he is sustained by nothing except his tyrannical insistence on his own will, come what may, and his outraged refusal to be defeated by a woman. "No woman," he says, "is going to lord it over me" (593). "I am not the man, not now: she is the man / if this victory goes to her and she goes free" (541–42).

Antigone, on her side, is just as indifferent to Creon's principles of action as he is to hers. She mentions the city only in her last agonized laments before she is led off to her living death:

> O my city, all your fine rich sons!
> ... springs of the Dirce,
> holy grove of Thebes ... (934–36)

But here she is appealing for sympathy to the city over the heads of the chorus, the city's symbolic representative on stage. In all her arguments with Creon and Ismene she speaks as one wholly unconscious of the rights and duties membership in the city confers and imposes, as if no unit larger than the family existed. It is a position just as extreme as Creon's insistence that the demands of the city take precedence over all others, for the living and the dead alike.

Like Creon, she acts in the name of gods, but they are different gods. There is more than a little truth in Creon's mocking comment that Hades is "the one god she worships" (875). She is from the beginning "much possessed by death"; together with Ismene she is the last survivor of a doomed family, burdened with such sorrow that she finds life hardly worth living. "Who on earth," she says to Creon, "alive in the midst of so much grief as I, / could fail to find his death a rich reward?" (516–18). She has performed the funeral rites for mother, father and her brother Eteocles:

> I washed you with my hands,
> I dressed you all, I poured the sacred cups
> across your tombs. (989–91)

She now sacrifices her life to perform a symbolic burial, a handful of dust sprinkled on the corpse, for Polynices, the brother left to rot on the battlefield. She looks forward to her reunion with her beloved dead in that dark kingdom where Persephone, the bride of Hades, welcomes the ghosts (980–82). It is in the name of Hades, one of the three great gods who rule the universe, that she defends the right of Polynices and of all human beings to proper burial. "Death [Hades] longs for the same rites for all" (584), she tells Creon—for patriot and traitor alike; she rejects Ismene's plea to be allowed to share her fate with an appeal to the same stern authority: "Who did the work? / Let the dead and the god of death bear witness!" (610–11). In Creon's gods, the city's patrons and defenders, she shows no interest at all. Zeus she mentions twice: once as the source of all the calamities that have fallen and are still to fall on the house of Oedipus (3–5), and once again at the beginning of her famous speech about the unwritten laws. But the context here suggests strongly that she is thinking about Zeus in his special relationship to the underworld, Zeus *Chthonios* (Underworld Zeus). "It wasn't Zeus," she says,

> who made this proclamation. . . .
> Nor did that Justice, dwelling with the gods
> beneath the earth, ordain such laws for men.   (499–502)

From first to last her religious devotion and duty are to the divine powers of the world below, the masters of that world where lie her family dead, to which she herself, reluctant but fascinated, is irresistibly drawn.

But, like Creon, she ends by denying the great sanctions she invoked to justify her action. In his case the process was spread out over the course of several scenes, as he reacted to each fresh pressure that was brought to bear on him; Antigone turns her back on the claims of blood relationship and the nether gods in one sentence: three lines in Greek, no more. They are the emotional high point of the speech she makes just before she is led off to her death.

> Never, I tell you,
> if I had been the mother of children
> or if my husband died, exposed and rotting—
> I'd never have taken this ordeal upon myself,
> never defied our people's will.   (995–99)

These unexpected words are part of the long speech that concludes a scene of lyric lamentation and is in effect her farewell to the land of the living. They are certainly a total repudiation of her proud claim that she acted as the champion of the unwritten laws and the infernal gods, for, as she herself told Creon, those laws and those gods have no preferences, they long "for the same rites for all" (584). And her assertion that she would not have done for her children what she has done for Polynices is a spectacular betrayal of that fanatical loyalty to blood relationship which she urged on Ismene and defended against Creon, for there is no closer relationship imaginable than that between the mother and the children of her own body. Creon turned his back on his guiding principles step by step, in reaction to opposition based on those principles; Antigone's rejection of her public values is just as complete, but it is the sudden product of a lonely, brooding introspection, a last-minute assessment of her motives, on which the imminence of death confers a merciless clarity. She did it because Polynices was her brother; she would not have done it for husband or child. She goes on to justify this disturbing statement by an argument which is more disturbing still: husband and children, she says, could be replaced by others but, since her parents are dead, she could never have another brother. It so happens that we can identify the source of this strange piece of reasoning; it is a story in the *Histories* of Sophocles' friend Herodotus (a work from which Sophocles borrowed material more than once). Darius the Great King had condemned to death for treason a Persian noble, Intaphrenes, and all the men of his family. The wife of Intaphrenes begged importunately for their lives; offered one, she chose her brother's. When Darius asked her why, she replied in words that are unmistakably the original of Antigone's lines. But what makes sense in the story makes less in the play. The wife of Intaphrenes saves her brother's life, but Polynices is already dead; Antigone's phrase "no brother could ever spring to light again" (1004) would be fully appropriate only if Antigone had managed to save Polynices' life rather than bury his corpse.

For this reason, and also because of some stylistic anomalies in this part of the speech, but most of all because they felt that the words are unworthy of the Antigone who spoke so nobly for the unwritten laws, many great scholars and also a great poet and dramatist, Goethe, have refused to believe that Sophocles wrote them. "I would give a great deal," Goethe told his friend Eckermann in 1827, "if some talented scholar could prove that these lines were interpolated, not genuine." Goethe did not know that the attempt had already been made, six years earlier; many others have tried since—Sir Richard Jebb, the greatest English editor of Sophocles, pronounced against them—and opinion today is still divided. Obviously a decision on this point is of vital significance for the interpretation of the play as a whole: with these lines removed, Antigone goes to her prison-tomb with no flicker of self-doubt, the flawless champion of the family bond and the unwritten laws, "whole as the marble, founded as the rock"— unlike Creon, she is not, in the end, reduced to recognizing that her motive is purely personal.

There is however one objective piece of evidence that speaks volumes for the authenticity of the disputed lines. Aristotle, writing his treatise on rhetoric less than a century after the death of Sophocles, summarizes this part of Antigone's speech and quotes the two lines about the irreplaceability of a brother. He is telling the would-be orator that if, in a law-court speech for the defense, he has to describe an action that seems inappropriate for the character of his client and hard to believe, he must provide an explanation for it "as in the example Sophocles gives, the one from *Antigone*"—the phrasing suggests that the passage was well known to Aristotle's readers. Evidently he does not find the passage as repellent as Goethe and Jebb did; he recognizes that Antigone's initial statement is, in terms of her character, "hard to believe" (*apiston*), but apparently he finds her explanation rhetorically satisfactory. He does not, however, for one moment suspect the authenticity of the lines. And this should make modern critics think twice before they make another attempt to oblige the shade of Goethe. Aristotle was head of a philosophical school which, under his direction, investigated the origins and early history of drama and drew up its chronology, based on official documents; he was himself the author of the most influential critique of the drama ever written, the *Poetics;* he was an acute critic of poetic style, with a keen eye for improprieties of diction and syntax; and, finally, he was perfectly conscious of the possibility of really damaging inconsistency of character, for in the *Poetics* he criticized Euripides' *Iphigenia in Aulis* on precisely that score. His acceptance of Antigone's speech as genuine demands that rather than suppress it we should try to understand it.

This is Antigone's third and last appearance on stage; in the prologue she planned her action, in the confrontation with Creon she defended it, and now, under guard, she is on her way to the prison which is to be her tomb. In lyric meters, the dramatic medium for unbridled emotion, she appeals to the chorus for sympathy and mourns for the marriage hymn she will never hear (this is as close as she ever comes to mentioning Haemon). She gets little comfort from the Theban elders; the only consolation they offer is a reminder that she may be the victim of a family curse—"do you pay for your father's terrible ordeal?" (946)—a suggestion that touches her to the quick and provokes a horror-struck rehearsal of the tormented loves and crimes of the house of Oedipus. There is, as she goes on to say, no one left to mourn her; the lyric lament she sings in this scene is her attempt to provide for herself that funeral dirge which her blood relatives would have wailed over her corpse, if they had not already preceded her into the realm of Hades. This is recognized by Creon, who cuts off the song with a sarcastic comment: "if a man could wail his own dirge *before* he dies, / he'd never finish" (970–71). And he orders the guards to take her away.

Her song cut off, she turns from the lyric medium of emotion to spoken verse, the vehicle of reasoned statement, for her farewell speech. It is not directed at anyone on stage; it resembles a soliloquy, a private meditation. It is an attempt to understand the real reasons for the action that has brought her to the brink of death. After an address to the tomb and prison where she expects to be reunited with her family she speaks to Polynices (Creon is referred to in the third person). It is to Polynices that she is speaking when she says that she would not have given her life for anyone but a brother; it is as if she had already left the world of the living and joined that community of the family dead she speaks of with such love. Now, in the face of death, oblivious of the presence of Creon and the chorus, with no public case to make, no arguments to counter, she can at last identify the driving force behind her action, the private, irrational imperative which was at the root of her championship of the rights of family and the dead against the demands of the state. It is her fanatical devotion to one particular family, her own, the doomed, incestuous, accursed house of Oedipus and especially to its most unfortunate member, the brother whose corpse lay exposed to the birds and dogs. When she tells him that she has done for him what she would not have done for husband or children she is not speaking in wholly hypothetical terms, for in sober fact she has sacrificed, for his sake, her marriage to Haemon and the children that might have issued from it.

And in this moment of self-discovery she realizes that she is absolutely alone, not only rejected by men but also abandoned by gods. "What law of the mighty gods have I transgressed?" (1013) she asks—as well she may, for whatever her motive may have been, her action was a blow struck for the rights of Hades and the dead. Unlike Christians whose master told them not to look for signs from heaven (Matthew 16:4), the ancient Greek expected if not direct intervention at least some manifestation of favor or support from his gods when he believed his cause was just—a flight of eagles, the bird of Zeus, or lightning and thunder, the signs which, in the last play, summon Oedipus to his resting place. But Antigone has to renounce this prospect: "Why look to the heavens any more . . . ?" (1014). She must go to her death as she has lived, alone, without a word of approval or a helping hand from men or gods.

Antigone's discovery that her deepest motives were purely personal has been overinterpreted by those who would suppress the passage on the grounds that, to quote Jebb's eloquent indictment, "she suddenly gives up that which, throughout the drama, has been the immovable basis of her action—the universal and unqualified validity of the divine law." This formulation is too absolute. Before the raw immediacy of death, which, as Doctor Johnson remarked, wonderfully concentrates the mind, she has sounded the depths of her own soul and identified the determinant of those high principles she proclaimed in public. But that does not mean that they were a pretense, still less that she has now abandoned them. She dies for them. In her very last words, as she calls on the chorus to bear witness to her unjust fate, she claims once more and for the last time that she is the champion of divine law—she suffers "all for reverence, my reverence for the gods!" (1034).

Unlike Creon, who after proclaiming the predominance of the city's interests rides roughshod over them, speaking and acting like a tyrant, who after extolling the city's gods dismisses Tiresias, their spokesman, with a blasphemous insult, Antigone does not betray the loyalties she spoke for. No word of compromise or surrender comes to her lips, no plea for mercy; she has nothing to say to Creon—in fact the last words of her speech are a prayer to the gods for his punishment. "But if these men are wrong"—she does not even name him—

> let them suffer
> nothing worse than they mete out to me—
> these masters of injustice!   (1019–21)

The chorus is appalled. "Still the same rough winds, the wild passion / raging through the girl" (1022–23). And Creon, in a fury, repeats his order to the guards to take her away, quickly. And this time there is no delay.

Antigone reaffirms the rightness of her action, despite the open disapproval of the chorus and the silent indifference of the gods; she has not changed—"still the same rough winds, the wild passion . . ." The chorus here restates the judgment it has passed on her earlier in the scene: "Your own blind will, your passion has destroyed you" (962). This is of course the verdict of a chorus that is clearly sympathetic to Creon's political program (and also afraid of his wrath), but it contains an element of truth. This young princess is a formidable being, a combination of cold resolve and fierce intensity. Unlike Anouilh's Antigone she has no tender emotions; except when she speaks to Polynices, she is all hard steel. Once she has made up her mind to act, no persuasion, no threat, not death itself can break her resolution. She will not yield a point or give an inch: "she hasn't learned," says the chorus, "to bend before adversity" (527)—and she never does. Those who oppose her will are met with contempt and defiance; friends who try to dissuade her are treated as enemies. Even when she despairs of the gods to whom she had looked for help, she does not waver; she goes to her death with a last disdainful insult to Creon: "see what I suffer now / at the hands of what breed of men" (1032–33).

This is a pattern of character and behavior which is found in other Sophoclean dramatic figures also; not only in the Oedipus of the other two plays but also in the protagonists of *Ajax, Electra* and *Philoctetes.* They are of course very different from each other, but they all have in common the same uncompromising determination, the same high sense of their own worth and a consequent quickness to take offense, the readiness to die rather than surrender—a heroic temper. This figure of the tragic hero, though it had a nonhuman predecessor in the Aeschylean Titan Prometheus and its origin in the great Achilles of the Homeric *Iliad,* seems, as far as we can tell from what remains of Attic tragedy, to have been a peculiarly Sophoclean creation. In his plays he explores time and again the destinies of human beings who refuse to recognize the limits imposed on the individual will by men and gods, and go to death or triumph, magnificently defiant to the last.

Antigone is such a heroic figure, and this is another of the ways in which she is different from Creon. Not only does Creon, unlike Antigone, betray in action the principles he claimed to stand for; he also, subjected to pressure that falls far short of the death Antigone is faced with, collapses in abject surrender. He was sure Antigone would give way when force was applied; he has seen "the stiffest stubborn wills / fall the hardest; the toughest iron . . . crack and shatter" (528–31)—but he is wrong. He is the one who is shattered. Tiresias tells him that he will lose a child of his own to death in return for the living being he has imprisoned in the tomb and the corpse he has kept in the sunlight. He hesitates: "I'm shaken, torn. / It's a dreadful thing to yield . . ." (1218–19). But yield he does. "What should I do?" he asks the chorus (1223) and they tell him: release Antigone, bury Polynices. But he arrives too late; Antigone, independent to the last, has chosen her own way to die—she has hanged herself in the tomb. Creon finds Haemon mourning his betrothed; the son spits in his father's face, tries to run him through with his sword and, failing, kills himself. Creon's wife, Eurydice, hearing the news, kills herself too, her last words a curse on her husband.

Creon, as we learned from his speech to Haemon earlier in the play, had his own idea of what a family should be. "That's what a man prays for: to produce good sons— / a household full of them, dutiful and attentive . . ." (715–16). His savage dismissal of the claims of that blood relationship Antigone stood for has been punished with exquisite appropriateness, in the destruction of his own family, the curses of his son and wife. Tiresias predicted that he would have to repay the gods below with a death—"one born of your own loins" (1184); the payment has been double, son and wife as well. The gods of the city whom he claimed to defend, have, through the medium of the blind seer, denounced his action, and the city he proposed to steer on a firm course is now, as Tiresias told him, threatened by the other cities whose dead were left to rot, like Polynices, outside the walls of Thebes (1201–5). He is revealed as a disastrous failure, both as head of a family and head of state, an offender against heaven and a man without family or friends, without the respect of his fellow-citizens. He may well describe himself as "no one. Nothing" (1446).

Antigone asked the gods to punish Creon if he was wrong, and they have. They have shown to all the world that her action was right. But she did not live to see her vindication. She took her own life and by that action sealed the doom and ensured the punishment of Creon. But the will of the gods remains mysterious; revealed partially, if at all, through prophets rejected and prophecies misunderstood, it is the insoluble riddle at the heart of Sophocles' tragic vision. The gods told Creon he was wrong, but it is noticeable that Tiresias, their spokesman, does not say Antigone was right, he does not praise her—in fact he does not mention her. Antigone was ready to admit, if the gods did not save her and she suffered death, that she was wrong (1017–18); these words suggest that she hanged herself not just to cut short the lingering agony of starvation and imprisonment but in a sort of existential despair. Why did the gods not save her, since they approved her action? Was it because her motives, even those she openly proclaimed, were too narrow—her total indifference to the city and its rights an offense to heaven? Because, to use Eliot's phrase, she "did the right thing for the wrong reason"? We are not told. Her death, which leads directly to the destruction of Creon's family, is a thread in a tragic web spun by powers who are beyond our comprehension. "Since the gods conceal all things divine," runs a fragment from a lost Sophoclean play, "you will never understand them, not though you go searching to the ends of the earth."

The gods do not praise Antigone, nor does anyone else in the play—except the young man who loves her so passionately that he cannot bear to live without her. Haemon tells his father what the Thebans are saying behind his back, the "murmurs in the dark" (775): that Antigone deserves not death but "a glowing crown of gold!" (782). Whether this is a true report (and the chorus does not praise Antigone even when they have been convinced that she was right) or just his own feelings attributed to others for the sake of his argument, it is a timely reminder of Antigone's heroic status. In the somber world of the play, against the background of so many sudden deaths and the dark mystery of the divine dispensation, her courage and steadfastness are a gleam of light; she is the embodiment of the only consolation tragedy can offer—that in certain heroic natures unmerited suffering and death can be met with a greatness of soul which, because it is purely human, brings honor to us all.

ANTIGONE

CHARACTERS

ANTIGONE
daughter of Oedipus and Jocasta

ISMENE
sister of Antigone

A CHORUS
of old Theban citizens and their LEADER

CREON
king of Thebes, uncle of Antigone and Ismene

A SENTRY

HAEMON
son of Creon and Eurydice

TIRESIAS
a blind prophet

A MESSENGER

EURYDICE
wife of Creon

Guards, attendants, and a boy

[Line numbers at the head of each page refer to the Greek text; those in the margin refer to the English translation.]

TIME AND SCENE: *The royal house of Thebes. It is still night, and the invading armies of Argos have just been driven from the city. Fighting on opposite sides, the sons of Oedipus, Eteocles and Polynices, have killed each other in combat. Their uncle,* CREON, *is now king of Thebes.*

Enter ANTIGONE, *slipping through the central doors of the palace. She motions to her sister,* ISMENE, *who follows her cautiously toward an altar at the center of the stage.*

ANTIGONE:
My own flesh and blood—dear sister, dear Ismene,
how many griefs our father Oedipus handed down!
Do you know one, I ask you, one grief
that Zeus will not perfect for the two of us
while we still live and breathe? There's nothing,   5
no pain—our lives are pain—no private shame,
no public disgrace, nothing I haven't seen
in your griefs and mine. And now this:
an emergency decree, they say, the Commander
has just now declared for all of Thebes.   10
What, haven't you heard? Don't you see?
The doom reserved for enemies
marches on the ones we love the most.

ISMENE:
Not I, I haven't heard a word, Antigone.
Nothing of loved ones,   15
no joy or pain has come my way, not since
the two of us were robbed of our two brothers,
both gone in a day, a double blow—
not since the armies of Argos vanished,
just this very night. I know nothing more,   20
whether our luck's improved or ruin's still to come.

ANTIGONE:
I thought so. That's why I brought you out here,
past the gates, so you could hear in private.

ISMENE:
What's the matter? Trouble, clearly . . .
you sound so dark, so grim.   25

ANTIGONE:
Why not? Our own brothers' burial!
Hasn't Creon graced one with all the rites,
disgraced the other? Eteocles, they say,
has been given full military honors,
rightly so—Creon has laid him in the earth   30
and he goes with glory down among the dead.
But the body of Polynices, who died miserably—
why, a city-wide proclamation, rumor has it,
forbids anyone to bury him, even mourn him.
He's to be left unwept, unburied, a lovely treasure   35
for birds that scan the field and feast to their heart's content.

Such, I hear, is the martial law our good Creon
lays down for you and me—yes, me, I tell you—
and he's coming here to alert the uninformed
in no uncertain terms,   40
and he won't treat the matter lightly. Whoever
disobeys in the least will die, his doom is sealed:
stoning to death inside the city walls!

There you have it. You'll soon show what you are,
worth your breeding, Ismene, or a coward—   45
for all your royal blood.

ISMENE:
My poor sister, if things have come to this,
who am I to make or mend them, tell me,
what good am I to you?

ANTIGONE:
Decide.

Will you share the labor, share the work?   *50*

ISMENE:
What work, what's the risk? What do you mean?

ANTIGONE:
Raising her hands.

Will you lift up his body with these bare hands
and lower it with me?

ISMENE:
What? You'd bury him—

when a law forbids the city?

ANTIGONE:
Yes!

He is my brother and—deny it as you will—   *55*
your brother too.
No one will ever convict me for a traitor.

ISMENE:
So desperate, and Creon has expressly—

ANTIGONE:
No,

he has no right to keep me from my own.

ISMENE:
Oh my sister, think—   60
think how our own father died, hated,
his reputation in ruins, driven on
by the crimes he brought to light himself
to gouge out his eyes with his own hands—
then mother . . . his mother and wife, both in one,   65
mutilating her life in the twisted noose—
and last, our two brothers dead in a single day,
both shedding their own blood, poor suffering boys,
battling out their common destiny hand-to-hand.

Now look at the two of us, left so alone . . .   70
think what a death we'll die, the worst of all
if we violate the laws and override
the fixed decree of the throne, its power—
we must be sensible. Remember we are women,
we're not born to contend with men. Then too,   75
we're underlings, ruled by much stronger hands,
so we must submit in this, and things still worse.

I, for one, I'll beg the dead to forgive me—
I'm forced, I have no choice—I must obey
the ones who stand in power. Why rush to extremes?   80
It's madness, madness.

ANTIGONE:
                    I won't insist,
no, even if you should have a change of heart,
I'd never welcome you in the labor, not with me.
So, do as you like, whatever suits you best—
I will bury him myself   85
And even if I die in the act, that death will be a glory.
I will lie with the one I love and loved by him—
an outrage sacred to the gods! I have longer
to please the dead than please the living here:
in the kingdom down below I'll lie forever.   90
Do as you like, dishonor the laws
the gods hold in honor.

ISMENE:
                    I'd do them no dishonor . . .
but defy the city? I have no strength for that.

ANTIGONE:
You have your excuses. I am on my way,
I will raise a mound for him, for my dear brother.   95

ISMENE:
Oh Antigone, you're so rash—I'm so afraid for you!

ANTIGONE:
Don't fear for me. Set your own life in order.

ISMENE:
Then don't, at least, blurt this out to anyone.
Keep it a secret. I'll join you in that, I promise.

ANTIGONE:
Dear god, shout it from the rooftops. I'll hate you   100
all the more for silence—tell the world!

ISMENE:
So fiery—and it ought to chill your heart.

ANTIGONE:
I know I please where I must please the most.

ISMENE:
Yes, if you can, but you're in love with impossibility.

ANTIGONE:
Very well then, once my strength gives out   105
I will be done at last.

ISMENE:
                    You're wrong from the start,
you're off on a hopeless quest.

ANTIGONE:
If you say so, you will make me hate you,
and the hatred of the dead, by all rights,
will haunt you night and day.   110
But leave me to my own absurdity, leave me
to suffer this—dreadful thing. I will suffer
nothing as great as death without glory.

                              Exit to the side.

ISMENE:
Then go if you must, but rest assured,
wild, irrational as you are, my sister,   115
you are truly dear to the ones who love you.

                         Withdrawing to the palace.

Enter a CHORUS, *the old citizens*
of Thebes, chanting as the sun begins
to rise.

CHORUS:
Glory!—great beam of the sun, brightest of all
that ever rose on the seven gates of Thebes,
   you burn through night at last!
       Great eye of the golden day,   120
mounting the Dirce's banks you throw him back—
the enemy out of Argos, the white shield, the man of bronze—
he's flying headlong now
       the bridle of fate stampeding him with pain!

    And he had driven against our borders,   125
    launched by the warring claims of Polynices—
    like an eagle screaming, winging havoc
    over the land, wings of armor
    shielded white as snow,
    a huge army massing,   130
    crested helmets bristling for assault.

He hovered above our roofs, his vast maw gaping
closing down around our seven gates,
   his spears thirsting for the kill
      but now he's gone, look,   135
before he could glut his jaws with Theban blood
or the god of fire put our crown of towers to the torch.
He grappled the Dragon none can master—Thebes—
      the clang of our arms like thunder at his back!

    Zeus hates with a vengeance all bravado,   140
    the mighty boasts of men. He watched them
    coming on in a rising flood, the pride
    of their golden armor ringing shrill—
    and brandishing his lightning
    blasted the fighter just at the goal,   145
    rushing to shout his triumph from our walls.

Down from the heights he crashed, pounding down on the earth!
And a moment ago, blazing torch in hand—
                    mad for attack, ecstatic
he breathed his rage, the storm   150
    of his fury hurling at our heads!
But now his high hopes have laid him low
and down the enemy ranks the iron god of war
          deals his rewards, his stunning blows—Ares
          rapture of battle, our right arm in the crisis.   155

          Seven captains marshaled at seven gates
          seven against their equals, gave
          their brazen trophies up to Zeus,
          god of the breaking rout of battle,
          all but two: those blood brothers,   160
          one father, one mother—matched in rage,
          spears matched for the twin conquest—
          clashed and won the common prize of death.

But now for Victory! Glorious in the morning,
joy in her eyes to meet our joy   165
    she is winging down to Thebes,
our fleets of chariots wheeling in her wake—
    Now let us win oblivion from the wars,
thronging the temples of the gods
in singing, dancing choirs through the night!   170
          Lord Dionysus, god of the dance
          that shakes the land of Thebes, now lead the way!

                              Enter CREON *from the palace,*
                              attended by his guard.

          But look, the king of the realm is coming,
          Creon, the new man for the new day,
          whatever the gods are sending now . . .   175
          what new plan will he launch?
          Why this, this special session?
          Why this sudden call to the old men
          summoned at one command?

CREON:

My countrymen,
the ship of state is safe. The gods who rocked her,   *180*
after a long, merciless pounding in the storm,
have righted her once more.

Out of the whole city
I have called you here alone. Well I know,
first, your undeviating respect
for the throne and royal power of King Laius.   *185*
Next, while Oedipus steered the land of Thebes,
and even after he died, your loyalty was unshakable,
you still stood by their children. Now then,
since the two sons are dead—two blows of fate
in the same day, cut down by each other's hands,   *190*
both killers, both brothers stained with blood—
as I am next in kin to the dead,
I now possess the throne and all its powers.

Of course you cannot know a man completely,
his character, his principles, sense of judgment,   *195*
not till he's shown his colors, ruling the people,
making laws. Experience, there's the test.
As I see it, whoever assumes the task,
the awesome task of setting the city's course,
and refuses to adopt the soundest policies   *200*
but fearing someone, keeps his lips locked tight,
he's utterly worthless. So I rate him now,
I always have. And whoever places a friend
above the good of his own country, he is nothing:
I have no use for him. Zeus my witness,   *205*
Zeus who sees all things, always—

I could never stand by silent, watching destruction
march against our city, putting safety to rout,
nor could I ever make that man a friend of mine
who menaces our country. Remember this: 210
our country *is* our safety.
Only while she voyages true on course
can we establish friendships, truer than blood itself.
Such are my standards. They make our city great.

Closely akin to them I have proclaimed,   215
just now, the following decree to our people
concerning the two sons of Oedipus.
Eteocles, who died fighting for Thebes,
excelling all in arms: he shall be buried,
crowned with a hero's honors, the cups we pour   220
to soak the earth and reach the famous dead.

But as for his blood brother, Polynices,
who returned from exile, home to his father-city
and the gods of his race, consumed with one desire—
to burn them roof to roots—who thirsted to drink   225
his kinsmen's blood and sell the rest to slavery:
that man—a proclamation has forbidden the city
to dignify him with burial, mourn him at all.
No, he must be left unburied, his corpse
carrion for the birds and dogs to tear,   230
an obscenity for the citizens to behold!

These are my principles. Never at my hands
will the traitor be honored above the patriot.
But whoever proves his loyalty to the state—
I'll prize that man in death as well as life.   235

LEADER:
If this is your pleasure, Creon, treating
our city's enemy and our friend this way . . .
The power is yours, I suppose, to enforce it
with the laws, both for the dead and all of us,
the living.

CREON:
           Follow my orders closely then,   240
be on your guard.

LEADER:
              We are too old.
Lay that burden on younger shoulders.

CREON:
                    No, no,
I don't mean the body—I've posted guards already.

LEADER:
What commands for us then? What other service?

CREON:
See that you never side with those who break my orders.   245

LEADER:
Never. Only a fool could be in love with death.

CREON:
Death is the price—you're right. But all too often
the mere hope of money has ruined many men.

A SENTRY *enters from the side.*

SENTRY:

My lord,
I can't say I'm winded from running, or set out
with any spring in my legs either—no sir,   250
I was lost in thought, and it made me stop, often,
dead in my tracks, wheeling, turning back,
and all the time a voice inside me muttering,
"Idiot, why? You're going straight to your death."
Then muttering, "Stopped again, poor fool?   255
If somebody gets the news to Creon first,
what's to save your neck?"
                         And so,
mulling it over, on I trudged, dragging my feet,
you can make a short road take forever . . .
but at last, look, common sense won out,   260
I'm here, and I'm all yours,
and even though I come empty-handed
I'll tell my story just the same, because
I've come with a good grip on one hope,
what will come will come, whatever fate—   265

CREON:
Come to the point!
What's wrong—why so afraid?

SENTRY:
First, myself, I've got to tell you,
I didn't do it, didn't see who did—
Be fair, don't take it out on me.   270

CREON:
You're playing it safe, soldier,
barricading yourself from any trouble.
It's obvious, you've something strange to tell.

SENTRY:
Dangerous too, and danger makes you delay
for all you're worth.   *275*

CREON:
Out with it—then dismiss!

SENTRY:
All right, here it comes. The body—
someone's just buried it, then run off . . .
sprinkled some dry dust on the flesh,
given it proper rites.

CREON:
                              What?   *280*
What man alive would dare—

SENTRY:
                                        I've no idea, I swear it.
There was no mark of a spade, no pickaxe there,
no earth turned up, the ground packed hard and dry,
unbroken, no tracks, no wheelruts, nothing,
the workman left no trace. Just at sunup   *285*
the first watch of the day points it out—
it was a wonder! We were stunned . . .
a terrific burden too, for all of us, listen:
you can't see the corpse, not that it's buried,
really, just a light cover of road-dust on it,   *290*
as if someone meant to lay the dead to rest
and keep from getting cursed.
Not a sign in sight that dogs or wild beasts
had worried the body, even torn the skin.

But what came next! Rough talk flew thick and fast,   295
guard grilling guard—we'd have come to blows
at last, nothing to stop it; each man for himself
and each the culprit, no one caught red-handed,
all of us pleading ignorance, dodging the charges,
ready to take up red-hot iron in our fists,   300
go through fire, swear oaths to the gods—
"I didn't do it, I had no hand in it either,
not in the plotting, not the work itself!"

Finally, after all this wrangling came to nothing,
one man spoke out and made us stare at the ground,   305
hanging our heads in fear. No way to counter him,
no way to take his advice and come through
safe and sound. Here's what he said:
"Look, we've got to report the facts to Creon,
we can't keep this hidden." Well, that won out,   310
and the lot fell to me, condemned me,
unlucky as ever, I got the prize. So here I am,
against my will and yours too, well I know—
no one wants the man who brings bad news.

LEADER:
                                             My king,
ever since he began I've been debating in my mind,   315
could this possibly be the work of the gods?

CREON:

                                Stop—
before you make me choke with anger—the gods!
You, you're senile, must you be insane?
You say—why it's intolerable—say the gods
could have the slightest concern for that corpse?					320
Tell me, was it for meritorious service
they proceeded to bury him, prized him so? The hero
who came to burn their temples ringed with pillars,
their golden treasures—scorch their hallowed earth
and fling their laws to the winds.					325
Exactly when did you last see the gods
celebrating traitors? Inconceivable!

No, from the first there were certain citizens
who could hardly stand the spirit of my regime,
grumbling against me in the dark, heads together,					330
tossing wildly, never keeping their necks beneath
the yoke, loyally submitting to their king.
These are the instigators, I'm convinced—
they've perverted my own guard, bribed them
to do their work.
                 Money! Nothing worse					335
in our lives, so current, rampant, so corrupting.
Money—you demolish cities, root men from their homes,
you train and twist good minds and set them on
to the most atrocious schemes. No limit,
you make them adept at every kind of outrage,					340
every godless crime—money!
                     Everyone—
the whole crew bribed to commit this crime,
they've made one thing sure at least:
sooner or later they will pay the price.

Wheeling on the SENTRY.

You—

I swear to Zeus as I still believe in Zeus,   345
if you don't find the man who buried that corpse,
the very man, and produce him before my eyes,
simple death won't be enough for you,
not till we string you up alive
and wring the immorality out of you.   350
Then you can steal the rest of your days,
better informed about where to make a killing.
You'll have learned, at last, it doesn't pay
to itch for rewards from every hand that beckons.
Filthy profits wreck most men, you'll see—   355
they'll never save your life.

SENTRY:

Please,

may I say a word or two, or just turn and go?

CREON:

Can't you tell? Everything you say offends me.

SENTRY:

Where does it hurt you, in the ears or in the heart?

CREON:

And who are you to pinpoint my displeasure?   360

SENTRY:

The culprit grates on your feelings,
I just annoy your ears.

CREON:

                          Still talking?
You talk too much! A born nuisance—

SENTRY:

                                         Maybe so,
but I never did this thing, so help me!

CREON:

                                    Yes you did—
what's more, you squandered your life for silver!   365

SENTRY:

Oh it's terrible when the one who does the judging
judges things all wrong.

CREON:

                          Well now,
you just be clever about your judgments—
if you fail to produce the criminals for me,
you'll swear your dirty money brought you pain.   370

                              Turning sharply, reentering
                              the palace.

SENTRY:

I hope he's found. Best thing by far.
But caught or not, that's in the lap of fortune:
I'll never come back, you've seen the last of me.
I'm saved, even now, and I never thought,
I never hoped—   375
dear gods, I owe you all my thanks!

Rushing out.

CHORUS:
                                        Numberless wonders
terrible wonders walk the world but none the match for man—
that great wonder crossing the heaving gray sea,
                        driven on by the blasts of winter
on through breakers crashing left and right,   380
    holds his steady course
and the oldest of the gods he wears away—
the Earth, the immortal, the inexhaustible—
as his plows go back and forth, year in, year out
    with the breed of stallions turning up the furrows.   385

And the blithe, lightheaded race of birds he snares,
the tribes of savage beasts, the life that swarms the depths—
                        with one fling of his nets
woven and coiled tight, he takes them all,
    man the skilled, the brilliant!   390
He conquers all, taming with his techniques
the prey that roams the cliffs and wild lairs,
training the stallion, clamping the yoke across
    his shaggy neck, and the tireless mountain bull.

And speech and thought, quick as the wind   395
and the mood and mind for law that rules the city—
   all these he has taught himself
and shelter from the arrows of the frost
when there's rough lodging under the cold clear sky
and the shafts of lashing rain—   400
      ready, resourceful man!
           Never without resources
never an impasse as he marches on the future—
only Death, from Death alone he will find no rescue
but from desperate plagues he has plotted his escapes.   405

Man the master, ingenious past all measure
past all dreams, the skills within his grasp—
   he forges on, now to destruction
now again to greatness. When he weaves in
the laws of the land, and the justice of the gods   410
that binds his oaths together
      he and his city rise high—
         but the city casts out
that man who weds himself to inhumanity
thanks to reckless daring. Never share my hearth   415
never think my thoughts, whoever does such things.

Enter ANTIGONE *from the side,*
accompanied by the SENTRY.

Here is a dark sign from the gods—
what to make of this? I know her,
how can I deny it? That young girl's Antigone!
Wretched, child of a wretched father,   420
Oedipus. Look, is it possible?
They bring you in like a prisoner—
why? did you break the king's laws?
Did they take you in some act of mad defiance?

SENTRY:
She's the one, she did it single-handed—   425
we caught her burying the body. Where's Creon?

Enter CREON *from the palace.*

LEADER:
Back again, just in time when you need him.

CREON:
In time for what? What is it?

SENTRY:

My king,
there's nothing you can swear you'll never do—
second thoughts make liars of us all.   430
I could have sworn I wouldn't hurry back
(what with your threats, the buffeting I just took),
but a stroke of luck beyond our wildest hopes,
what a joy, there's nothing like it. So,
back I've come, breaking my oath, who cares?   435
I'm bringing in our prisoner—this young girl—
we took her giving the dead the last rites.
But no casting lots this time; this is *my* luck,
my prize, no one else's.

Now, my lord,
here she is. Take her, question her,   440
cross-examine her to your heart's content.
But set me free, it's only right—
I'm rid of this dreadful business once for all.

CREON:

Prisoner! Her? You took her—where, doing what?

SENTRY:

Burying the man. That's the whole story.

CREON:

What?   445
You mean what you say, you're telling me the truth?

SENTRY:

She's the one. With my own eyes I saw her
bury the body, just what you've forbidden.
There. Is that plain and clear?

CREON:
What did you see? Did you catch her in the act?   450

SENTRY:
Here's what happened. We went back to our post,
those threats of yours breathing down our necks—
we brushed the corpse clean of the dust that covered it,
stripped it bare . . . it was slimy, going soft,
and we took to high ground, backs to the wind   455
so the stink of him couldn't hit us;
jostling, baiting each other to keep awake,
shouting back and forth—no napping on the job,
not this time. And so the hours dragged by
until the sun stood dead above our heads,   460
a huge white ball in the noon sky, beating,
blazing down, and then it happened—
suddenly, a whirlwind!
Twisting a great dust-storm up from the earth,
a black plague of the heavens, filling the plain,   465
ripping the leaves off every tree in sight,
choking the air and sky. We squinted hard
and took our whipping from the gods.

And after the storm passed—it seemed endless—
there, we saw the girl!   470
And she cried out a sharp, piercing cry,
like a bird come back to an empty nest,
peering into its bed, and all the babies gone . . .
Just so, when she sees the corpse bare
she bursts into a long, shattering wail   475
and calls down withering curses on the heads
of all who did the work. And she scoops up dry dust,
handfuls, quickly, and lifting a fine bronze urn,
lifting it high and pouring, she crowns the dead
with three full libations.

                    Soon as we saw   480
we rushed her, closed on the kill like hunters,
and she, she didn't flinch. We interrogated her,
charging her with offenses past and present—
she stood up to it all, denied nothing. I tell you,
it made me ache and laugh in the same breath.   485
It's pure joy to escape the worst yourself,
it hurts a man to bring down his friends.
But all that, I'm afraid, means less to me
than my own skin. That's the way I'm made.

CREON:

                              Wheeling on ANTIGONE.

                                        You,
with your eyes fixed on the ground—speak up.   490
Do you deny you did this, yes or no?

ANTIGONE:
I did it. I don't deny a thing.

CREON:

                         To the SENTRY.
You, get out, wherever you please—
you're clear of a very heavy charge.

                         He leaves; CREON *turns back to*
                         ANTIGONE.

You, tell me briefly, no long speeches—   495
were you aware a decree had forbidden this?

ANTIGONE:
Well aware. How could I avoid it? It was public.

CREON:
And still you had the gall to break this law?

ANTIGONE:
Of course I did. It wasn't Zeus, not in the least,
who made this proclamation—not to me.   500
Nor did that Justice, dwelling with the gods
beneath the earth, ordain such laws for men.
Nor did I think your edict had such force
that you, a mere mortal, could override the gods,
the great unwritten, unshakable traditions.   505
They are alive, not just today or yesterday:
they live forever, from the first of time,
and no one knows when they first saw the light.

These laws—I was not about to break them,
not out of fear of some man's wounded pride,   510
and face the retribution of the gods.
Die I must, I've known it all my life—
how could I keep from knowing?—even without
your death-sentence ringing in my ears.
And if I am to die before my time   515
I consider that a gain. Who on earth,
alive in the midst of so much grief as I,
could fail to find his death a rich reward?
So for me, at least, to meet this doom of yours
is precious little pain. But if I had allowed   520
my own mother's son to rot, an unburied corpse—
that would have been an agony! This is nothing.
And if my present actions strike you as foolish,
let's just say I've been accused of folly
by a fool.

LEADER:
                    Like father like daughter,   525
passionate, wild . . .
she hasn't learned to bend before adversity.

CREON:
No? Believe me, the stiffest stubborn wills
fall the hardest; the toughest iron,
tempered strong in the white-hot fire,　　　　　*530*
you'll see it crack and shatter first of all.
And I've known spirited horses you can break
with a light bit—proud, rebellious horses.
There's no room for pride, not in a slave,
not with the lord and master standing by.　　　　　*535*

This girl was an old hand at insolence
when she overrode the edicts we made public.
But once she had done it—the insolence,
twice over—to glory in it, laughing,
mocking us to our face with what she'd done.　　　　　*540*
I am not the man, not now: she is the man
if this victory goes to her and she goes free.

Never! Sister's child or closer in blood
than all my family clustered at my altar
worshiping Guardian Zeus—she'll never escape,　　　　　*545*
she and her blood sister, the most barbaric death.
Yes, I accuse her sister of an equal part
in scheming this, this burial.

To his attendants.

Bring her here!
I just saw her inside, hysterical, gone to pieces.
It never fails: the mind convicts itself　　　　　*550*
in advance, when scoundrels are up to no good,
plotting in the dark. Oh but I hate it more
when a traitor, caught red-handed,
tries to glorify his crimes.

ANTIGONE:
Creon, what more do you want　　　　　*555*
than my arrest and execution?

CREON:
Nothing. Then I have it all.

ANTIGONE:
Then why delay? Your moralizing repels me,
every word you say—pray god it always will.
So naturally all I say repels you too.

                                    Enough.   560
Give me glory! What greater glory could I win
than to give my own brother decent burial?
These citizens here would all agree,

                    To the CHORUS.

they would praise me too
if their lips weren't locked in fear.   565

                    Pointing to CREON.

Lucky tyrants—the perquisites of power!
Ruthless power to do and say whatever pleases *them*.

CREON:
You alone, of all the people in Thebes,
see things that way.

ANTIGONE:
                    They see it just that way
but defer to you and keep their tongues in leash.   570

CREON:
And you, aren't you ashamed to differ so from them?
So disloyal!

ANTIGONE:
                    Not ashamed for a moment,
not to honor my brother, my own flesh and blood.

CREON:
Wasn't Eteocles a brother too—cut down, facing him?

ANTIGONE:
Brother, yes, by the same mother, the same father.   575

CREON:
Then how can you render his enemy such honors,
such impieties in his eyes?

ANTIGONE:
He will never testify to that,
Eteocles dead and buried.

CREON:
                                    He will—
if you honor the traitor just as much as him.   580

ANTIGONE:
But it was his brother, not some slave that died—

CREON:
Ravaging our country!—
but Eteocles died fighting in our behalf.

ANTIGONE:
No matter—Death longs for the same rites for all.

CREON:
Never the same for the patriot and the traitor.   585

ANTIGONE:
Who, Creon, who on earth can say the ones below
don't find this pure and uncorrupt?

CREON:

Never. Once an enemy, never a friend,
not even after death.

ANTIGONE:

I was born to join in love, not hate—   590
that is my nature.

CREON:

                    Go down below and love,
if love you must—love the dead! While I'm alive,
no woman is going to lord it over me.

                              Enter ISMENE *from the palace,*
                              under guard.

CHORUS:

                                        Look,
Ismene's coming, weeping a sister's tears,
loving sister, under a cloud . . .   595
her face is flushed, her cheeks streaming.
Sorrow puts her lovely radiance in the dark.

CREON:

                                        You—
in my own house, you viper, slinking undetected,
sucking my life-blood! I never knew
I was breeding twin disasters, the two of you   600
rising up against my throne. Come, tell me,
will you confess your part in the crime or not?
Answer me. Swear to me.

ISMENE:

                        I did it, yes—
if only she consents—I share the guilt,
the consequences too.

ANTIGONE:
/   No,   605
Justice will never suffer that—not you,
you were unwilling. I never brought you in.

ISMENE:
But now you face such dangers . . . I'm not ashamed
to sail through trouble with you,
make your troubles mine.

ANTIGONE:
                              Who did the work?   610
Let the dead and the god of death bear witness!
I have no love for a friend who loves in words alone.

ISMENE:
Oh no, my sister, don't reject me, please,
let me die beside you, consecrating
the dead together.

ANTIGONE:
                        Never share my dying,   615
don't lay claim to what you never touched.
My death will be enough.

ISMENE:
What do I care for life, cut off from you?

ANTIGONE:
Ask Creon. Your concern is all for him.

ISMENE:
Why abuse me so? It doesn't help you now.

ANTIGONE:

You're right—   620

if I mock you, I get no pleasure from it,
only pain.

ISMENE:

Tell me, dear one,
what can I do to help you, even now?

ANTIGONE:

Save yourself. I don't grudge you your survival.

ISMENE:

Oh no, no, denied my portion in your death?   625

ANTIGONE:

You chose to live, I chose to die.

ISMENE:

Not, at least,
without every kind of caution I could voice.

ANTIGONE:

Your wisdom appealed to one world—mine, another.

ISMENE:

But look, we're both guilty, both condemned to death.

ANTIGONE:

Courage! Live your life. I gave myself to death,   630
long ago, so I might serve the dead.

CREON:

They're both mad, I tell you, the two of them.
One's just shown it, the other's been that way
since she was born.

ISMENE:
                    True, my king,
the sense we were born with cannot last forever . . .   635
commit cruelty on a person long enough
and the mind begins to go.

CREON:
                         Yours did,
when you chose to commit your crimes with her.

ISMENE:
How can I live alone, without her?

CREON:
                              Her?
Don't even mention her—she no longer exists.   640

ISMENE:
What? You'd kill your own son's bride?

CREON:
                              Absolutely:
there are other fields for him to plow.

ISMENE:
                              Perhaps,
but never as true, as close a bond as theirs.

CREON:
A worthless woman for my son? It repels me.

ISMENE:
Dearest Haemon, your father wrongs you so!   645

CREON:
Enough, enough—you and your talk of marriage!

ISMENE:
Creon—you're really going to rob your son of Antigone?

CREON:
Death will do it for me—break their marriage off.

LEADER:
So, it's settled then? Antigone must die?

CREON:
Settled, yes—we both know that.   650

To the guards.

Stop wasting time. Take them in.
From now on they'll act like women.
Tie them up, no more running loose;
even the bravest will cut and run,
once they see Death coming for their lives.   655

582–603] ANTIGONE

The guards escort ANTIGONE *and*
ISMENE *into the palace.* CREON
*remains while the old citizens form
their* CHORUS.

CHORUS:
Blest, they are the truly blest who all their lives
have never tasted devastation. For others, once
the gods have rocked a house to its foundations
   the ruin will never cease, cresting on and on
from one generation on throughout the race—   660
like a great mounting tide
driven on by savage northern gales,
       surging over the dead black depths
roiling up from the bottom dark heaves of sand
and the headlands, taking the storm's onslaught full-force,   665
roar, and the low moaning
               echoes on and on
                      and now
as in ancient times I see the sorrows of the house,
the living heirs of the old ancestral kings,
piling on the sorrows of the dead
   and one generation cannot free the next—   670
some god will bring them crashing down,
the race finds no release.
And now the light, the hope
       springing up from the late last root
in the house of Oedipus, that hope's cut down in turn   675
by the long, bloody knife swung by the gods of death
by a senseless word
            by fury at the heart.

                                            Zeus,
yours is the power, Zeus, what man on earth
can override it, who can hold it back?
Power that neither Sleep, the all-ensnaring   680
    no, nor the tireless months of heaven
can ever overmaster—young through all time,
mighty lord of power, you hold fast
    the dazzling crystal mansions of Olympus.
And throughout the future, late and soon   685
as through the past, your law prevails:
no towering form of greatness
    enters into the lives of mortals
                        free and clear of ruin.
                                            True,
our dreams, our high hopes voyaging far and wide   690
bring sheer delight to many, to many others
    delusion, blithe, mindless lusts
and the fraud steals on one slowly . . . unaware
till he trips and puts his foot into the fire.
    He was a wise old man who coined   695
the famous saying: "Sooner or later
foul is fair, fair is foul
to the man the gods will ruin"—
    He goes his way for a moment only
                        free of blinding ruin.   700

                    Enter HAEMON *from the palace.*

    Here's Haemon now, the last of all your sons.
    Does he come in tears for his bride,
    his doomed bride, Antigone—
    bitter at being cheated of their marriage?

CREON:
We'll soon know, better than seers could tell us.   705

Turning to HAEMON.

Son, you've heard the final verdict on your bride?
Are you coming now, raving against your father?
Or do you love me, no matter what I do?

HAEMON:
Father, I'm your *son* . . . you in your wisdom
set my bearings for me—I obey you.   710
No marriage could ever mean more to me than you,
whatever good direction you may offer.

CREON:
                              Fine, Haemon.
That's how you ought to feel within your heart,
subordinate to your father's will in every way.
That's what a man prays for: to produce good sons—   715
a household full of them, dutiful and attentive,
so they can pay his enemy back with interest
and match the respect their father shows his friend.
But the man who rears a brood of useless children,
what has he brought into the world, I ask you?   720
Nothing but trouble for himself, and mockery
from his enemies laughing in his face.
                              Oh Haemon,
never lose your sense of judgment over a woman.
The warmth, the rush of pleasure, it all goes cold
in your arms, I warn you . . . a worthless woman   725
in your house, a misery in your bed.
What wound cuts deeper than a loved one
turned against you? Spit her out,
like a mortal enemy—let the girl go.
Let her find a husband down among the dead.   730

Imagine it: I caught her in naked rebellion,
the traitor, the only one in the whole city.
I'm not about to prove myself a liar,
not to my people, no, I'm going to kill her!
That's right—so let her cry for mercy, sing her hymns   735
to Zeus who defends all bonds of kindred blood.
Why, if I bring up my own kin to be rebels,
think what I'd suffer from the world at large.
Show me the man who rules his household well:
I'll show you someone fit to rule the state.   740
That good man, my son,
I have every confidence he and he alone
can give commands and take them too. Staunch
in the storm of spears he'll stand his ground,
a loyal, unflinching comrade at your side.   745

But whoever steps out of line, violates the laws
or presumes to hand out orders to his superiors,
he'll win no praise from me. But that man
the city places in authority, his orders
must be obeyed, large and small,   750
right and wrong.
                  Anarchy—
show me a greater crime in all the earth!
She, she destroys cities, rips up houses,
breaks the ranks of spearmen into headlong rout.
But the ones who last it out, the great mass of them   755
owe their lives to discipline. Therefore
we must defend the men who live by law,
never let some woman triumph over us.
Better to fall from power, if fall we must,
at the hands of a man—never be rated   760
inferior to a woman, never.

LEADER:
                  To us,
unless old age has robbed us of our wits,
you seem to say what you have to say with sense.

HAEMON:
Father, only the gods endow a man with reason,
the finest of all their gifts, a treasure.   765
Far be it from me—I haven't the skill,
and certainly no desire, to tell you when,
if ever, you make a slip in speech . . . though
someone else might have a good suggestion.

Of course it's not for you,   770
in the normal run of things, to watch
whatever men say or do, or find to criticize.
The man in the street, you know, dreads your glance,
he'd never say anything displeasing to your face.
But it's for me to catch the murmurs in the dark,   775
the way the city mourns for this young girl.
"No woman," they say, "ever deserved death less,
and such a brutal death for such a glorious action.
She, with her own dear brother lying in his blood—
she couldn't bear to leave him dead, unburied,   780
food for the wild dogs or wheeling vultures.
Death? She deserves a glowing crown of gold!"
So they say, and the rumor spreads in secret,
darkly . . .
                    I rejoice in your success, father—
nothing more precious to me in the world.   785
What medal of honor brighter to his children
than a father's growing glory? Or a child's
to his proud father? Now don't, please,
be quite so single-minded, self-involved,
or assume the world is wrong and you are right.   790
Whoever thinks that he alone possesses intelligence,
the gift of eloquence, he and no one else,
and character too . . . such men, I tell you,
spread them open—you will find them empty.

                 No,
it's no disgrace for a man, even a wise man,   795
to learn many things and not to be too rigid.
You've seen trees by a raging winter torrent,
how many sway with the flood and salvage every twig,
but not the stubborn—they're ripped out, roots and all.
Bend or break. The same when a man is sailing: 800
haul your sheets too taut, never give an inch,
you'll capsize, and go the rest of the voyage
keel up and the rowing-benches under.

Oh give way. Relax your anger—change!
I'm young, I know, but let me offer this: 805
it would be best by far, I admit,
if a man were born infallible, right by nature.
If not—and things don't often go that way,
it's best to learn from those with good advice.

LEADER:
You'd do well, my lord, if he's speaking to the point,   810
to learn from him,

                Turning to HAEMON.

            and you, my boy, from him.
You both are talking sense.

CREON:
                So,
men our age, we're to be lectured, are we?—
schooled by a boy his age?

HAEMON:
Only in what is right. But if I seem young,   815
look less to my years and more to what I do

CREON:
Do? Is admiring rebels an achievement?

HAEMON:
I'd never suggest that you admire treason.

CREON:
                                        Oh?—
isn't that just the sickness that's attacked her?

HAEMON:
The whole city of Thebes denies it, to a man.   820

CREON:
And is Thebes about to tell me how to rule?

HAEMON:
Now, you see? Who's talking like a child?

CREON:
Am I to rule this land for others—or myself?

HAEMON:
It's no city at all, owned by one man alone.

CREON:
What? The city *is* the king's—that's the law!   825

HAEMON:
What a splendid king you'd make of a desert island—
you and you alone.

CREON:
                    To the CHORUS.
            This boy, I do believe,
is fighting on her side, the woman's side.

HAEMON:
If you are a woman, yes—
my concern is all for you.   830

CREON:
Why, you degenerate—bandying accusations,
threatening me with justice, your own father!

HAEMON:
I see my father offending justice—wrong.

CREON:
                                        Wrong?
To protect my royal rights?

HAEMON:
                          Protect your rights?
When you trample down the honors of the gods?   835

CREON:
You, you soul of corruption, rotten through—
woman's accomplice!

HAEMON:
                    That may be,
but you will never find me accomplice to a criminal.

CREON:
That's what *she* is,
and every word you say is a blatant appeal for her—   840

HAEMON:
And you, and me, and the gods beneath the earth.

CREON:
You will never marry her, not while she's alive.

HAEMON:
Then she will die . . . but her death will kill another.

CREON:
What, brazen threats? You go too far!

HAEMON:

What threat?
Combating your empty, mindless judgments with a word?   845

CREON:
You'll suffer for your sermons, you and your empty wisdom!

HAEMON:
If you weren't my father, I'd say you were insane.

CREON:
Don't flatter me with Father—you woman's slave!

HAEMON:
You really expect to fling abuse at me
and not receive the same?

CREON:
Is that so!   850
Now, by heaven, I promise you, you'll pay—
taunting, insulting me! Bring her out,
that hateful—she'll die now, here,
in front of his eyes, beside her groom!

HAEMON:
No, no, she will never die beside me—   855
don't delude yourself And you will never
see me, never set eyes on my face again.
Rage your heart out, rage with friends
who can stand the sight of you.
                              Rushing out.

LEADER:
Gone, my king, in a burst of anger.   860
A temper young as his . . . hurt him once,
he may do something violent.

CREON:
                                    Let him do—
dream up something desperate, past all human limit!
Good riddance. Rest assured,
he'll never save those two young girls from death.   865

LEADER:
Both of them, you really intend to kill them both?

CREON:
No, not her, the one whose hands are clean—
you're quite right.

LEADER:
                        But Antigone—
what sort of death do you have in mind for her?

CREON:
I will take her down some wild, desolate path   870
never trod by men, and wall her up alive
in a rocky vault, and set out short rations,
just the measure piety demands
to keep the entire city free of defilement.
There let her pray to the one god she worships: 875
Death—who knows?—may just reprieve her from death.
Or she may learn at last, better late than never,
what a waste of breath it is to worship Death.

                        Exit to the palace.

CHORUS:
Love, never conquered in battle
Love the plunderer laying waste the rich!   880
Love standing the night-watch
               guarding a girl's soft cheek,
you range the seas, the shepherds' steadings off in the wilds—
not even the deathless gods can flee your onset,
nothing human born for a day—   885
whoever feels your grip is driven mad.

                         Love!—
you wrench the minds of the righteous into outrage,
swerve them to their ruin—you have ignited this,
this kindred strife, father and son at war
                   and Love alone the victor—   890
warm glance of the bride triumphant, burning with desire!
Throned in power, side-by-side with the mighty laws!
Irresistible Aphrodite, never conquered—
Love, you mock us for your sport.

                         ANTIGONE *is brought from the palace*
                         under guard.

But now, even I would rebel against the king,   895
I would break all bounds when I see this—
I fill with tears, I cannot hold them back,
not any more . . . I see Antigone make her way
to the bridal vault where all are laid to rest.

ANTIGONE:

Look at me, men of my fatherland,   900
    setting out on the last road
looking into the last light of day
the last I will ever see . . .
the god of death who puts us all to bed
takes me down to the banks of Acheron alive—   905
    denied my part in the wedding-songs,
no wedding-song in the dusk has crowned my marriage—
I go to wed the lord of the dark waters.

CHORUS:

        Not crowned with glory or with a dirge,
        you leave for the deep pit of the dead.   910
        No withering illness laid you low,
        no strokes of the sword—a law to yourself,
        alone, no mortal like you, ever, you go down
        to the halls of Death alive and breathing.

ANTIGONE:

But think of Niobe—well I know her story—   915
    think what a living death she died,
Tantalus' daughter, stranger queen from the east:
there on the mountain heights, growing stone
binding as ivy, slowly walled her round
and the rains will never cease, the legends say   920
the snows will never leave her . . .
    wasting away, under her brows the tears
showering down her breasting ridge and slopes—
a rocky death like hers puts me to sleep.

CHORUS:

        But she was a god, born of gods,   925
        and we are only mortals born to die.
        And yet, of course, it's a great thing
        for a dying girl to hear, even to hear
        she shares a destiny equal to the gods,
        during life and later, once she's dead.

ANTIGONE:

                              O you mock me!
Why, in the name of all my fathers' gods
why can't you wait till I am gone—
     must you abuse me to my face?
O my city, all your fine rich sons!
And you, you springs of the Dirce,   935
holy grove of Thebes where the chariots gather,
          you at least, you'll bear me witness, look,
unmourned by friends and forced by such crude laws
I go to my rockbound prison, strange new tomb—
     always a stranger, O dear god,   940
     I have no home on earth and none below,
       not with the living, not with the breathless dead.

CHORUS:
          You went too far, the last limits of daring—
          smashing against the high throne of Justice!
             Your life's in ruins, child—I wonder . . .   945
          do you pay for your father's terrible ordeal?

ANTIGONE:
There—at last you've touched it, the worst pain
the worst anguish! Raking up the grief for father
     three times over, for all the doom
that's struck us down, the brilliant house of Laius.   950
O mother, your marriage-bed
the coiling horrors, the coupling there—
     you with your own son, my father—doomstruck mother!
Such, such were my parents, and I their wretched child.
I go to them now, cursed, unwed, to share their home—   955
     I am a stranger! O dear brother, doomed
     in your marriage—your marriage murders mine,
       your dying drags me down to death alive!

Enter Creon.

CHORUS:

> Reverence asks some reverence in return—
> but attacks on power never go unchecked,   960
>   not by the man who holds the reins of power.
> Your own blind will, your passion has destroyed you.

ANTIGONE:

> No one to weep for me, my friends,
> no wedding-song—they take me away
> in all my pain . . . the road lies open, waiting.   965
> Never again, the law forbids me to see
> the sacred eye of day. I am agony!
> No tears for the destiny that's mine,
> no loved one mourns my death.

CREON:

>   Can't you see?
> If a man could wail his own dirge *before* he dies,   970
> he'd never finish.

>   *To the guards.*

>   Take her away, quickly!
> Wall her up in the tomb, you have your orders.
> Abandon her there, alone, and let her choose—
> death or a buried life with a good roof for shelter.
> As for myself, my hands are clean. This young girl—   975
> dead or alive, she will be stripped of her rights,
> her stranger's rights, here in the world above.

ANTIGONE:
O tomb, my bridal-bed—my house, my prison
cut in the hollow rock, my everlasting watch!
I'll soon be there, soon embrace my own,   *980*
the great growing family of our dead
Persephone has received among her ghosts.

                                                    I,
the last of them all, the most reviled by far,
go down before my destined time's run out.
But still I go, cherishing one good hope: *985*
my arrival may be dear to father,
dear to you, my mother,
dear to you, my loving brother, Eteocles—
When you died I washed you with my hands,
I dressed you all, I poured the sacred cups   *990*
across your tombs. But now, Polynices,
because I laid your body out as well,
this, this is my reward. Nevertheless
I honored you—the decent will admit it—
well and wisely too.

                        Never, I tell you.   *995*
if I had been the mother of children
or if my husband died, exposed and rotting—
I'd never have taken this ordeal upon myself,
never defied our people's will. What law,
you ask, do I satisfy with what I say?   *1000*
A husband dead, there might have been another.
A child by another too, if I had lost the first.
But mother and father both lost in the halls of Death,
no brother could ever spring to light again.

For this law alone I held you first in honor.   1005
For this, Creon, the king, judges me a criminal
guilty of dreadful outrage, my dear brother!
And now he leads me off, a captive in his hands,
with no part in the bridal-song, the bridal-bed,
denied all joy of marriage, raising children—   1010
deserted so by loved ones, struck by fate,
I descend alive to the caverns of the dead.

What law of the mighty gods have I transgressed?
Why look to the heavens any more, tormented as I am?
Whom to call, what comrades now? Just think,   1015
my reverence only brands me for irreverence!
Very well: if this is the pleasure of the gods,
once I suffer I will know that I was wrong.
But if these men are wrong, let them suffer
nothing worse than they mete out to me—   1020
these masters of injustice!

LEADER:
Still the same rough winds, the wild passion
raging through the girl.

CREON:

To the guards.

Take her away.

You're wasting time—you'll pay for it too.

ANTIGONE:

Oh god, the voice of death. It's come, it's here.	*1025*

CREON:

True. Not a word of hope—your doom is sealed.

ANTIGONE:

Land of Thebes, city of all my fathers—
O you gods, the first gods of the race!
They drag me away, now, no more delay.
Look on me, you noble sons of Thebes—	*1030*
the last of a great line of kings,
I alone, see what I suffer now
at the hands of what breed of men—
all for reverence, my reverence for the gods!

She leaves under guard: the CHORUS
gathers.

CHORUS:
        Danaë, Danaë—   1035
even she endured a fate like yours,
    in all her lovely strength she traded
the light of day for the bolted brazen vault—
buried within her tomb, her bridal-chamber,
wed to the yoke and broken.   1040
        But she was of glorious birth
                            my child, my child
and treasured the seed of Zeus within her womb,
the cloudburst streaming gold!
        The power of fate is a wonder,   1045
        dark, terrible wonder—
        neither wealth nor armies
        towered walls nor ships
        black hulls lashed by the salt
        can save us from that force.   1050

The yoke tamed him too
    young Lycurgus flaming in anger
king of Edonia, all for his mad taunts
Dionysus clamped him down, encased
in the chain-mail of rock   1055
    and there his rage
            his terrible flowering rage burst—
sobbing, dying away . . . at last that madman
came to know his god—
        the power he mocked, the power   1060
        he taunted in all his frenzy
        trying to stamp out
        the women strong with the god—
        the torch, the raving sacred cries—
        enraging the Muses who adore the flute.   1065

And far north where the Black Rocks
        cut the sea in half
and murderous straits
split the coast of Thrace
    a forbidding city stands   1070
where once, hard by the walls
the savage Ares thrilled to watch
a king's new queen, a Fury rearing in rage
        against his two royal sons—
            her bloody hands, her dagger-shuttle   1075
stabbing out their eyes—cursed, blinding wounds—
their eyes blind sockets screaming for revenge!

They wailed in agony, cries echoing cries
        the princes doomed at birth . . .
and their mother doomed to chains,   1080
walled up in a tomb of stone—
    but she traced her own birth back
to a proud Athenian line and the high gods
and off in caverns half the world away,
born of the wild North Wind   1085
    she sprang on her father's gales,
        racing stallions up the leaping cliffs—
child of the heavens. But even on her the Fates
the gray everlasting Fates rode hard
my child, my child.

Enter TIRESIAS, *the blind prophet,*
led by a boy.

TIRESIAS:

                    Lords of Thebes   1090
I and the boy have come together,
hand in hand. Two see with the eyes of one . . .
so the blind must go, with a guide to lead the way.

CREON:
What is it, old Tiresias? What news now?

TIRESIAS:
I will teach you. And you obey the seer.

CREON:
                                   I will,   1095
I've never wavered from your advice before.

TIRESIAS:
And so you kept the city straight on course.

CREON:
I owe you a great deal, I swear to that.

TIRESIAS:
Then reflect, my son: you are poised,
once more, on the razor-edge of fate.   1100

CREON:
What is it? I shudder to hear you.

TIRESIAS:

You will learn
when you listen to the warnings of my craft.
As I sat on the ancient seat of augury,
in the sanctuary where every bird I know
will hover at my hands—suddenly I heard it,   1105
a strange voice in the wingbeats, unintelligible,
barbaric, a mad scream! Talons flashing, ripping,
they were killing each other—that much I knew—
the murderous fury whirring in those wings
made that much clear!

I was afraid,   1110
I turned quickly, tested the burnt-sacrifice,
ignited the altar at all points—but no fire,
the god in the fire never blazed.
Not from those offerings . . . over the embers
slid a heavy ooze from the long thighbones,   1115
smoking, sputtering out, and the bladder
puffed and burst—spraying gall into the air—
and the fat wrapping the bones slithered off
and left them glistening white. No fire!
The rites failed that might have blazed the future   1120
with a sign. So I learned from the boy here:
he is my guide, as I am guide to others.

And it is you—
your high resolve that sets this plague on Thebes.
The public altars and sacred hearths are fouled,
one and all, by the birds and dogs with carrion   1125
torn from the corpse, the doomstruck son of Oedipus!
And so the gods are deaf to our prayers, they spurn
the offerings in our hands, the flame of holy flesh.
No birds cry out an omen clear and true—
they're gorged with the murdered victim's blood and fat.   1130

Take these things to heart, my son, I warn you.
All men make mistakes, it is only human.
But once the wrong is done, a man
can turn his back on folly, misfortune too,
if he tries to make amends, however low he's fallen,   1135
and stops his bullnecked ways. Stubbornness
brands you for stupidity—pride is a crime.
No, yield to the dead!
Never stab the fighter when he's down.
Where's the glory, killing the dead twice over?   1140

I mean you well. I give you sound advice.
It's best to learn from a good adviser
when he speaks for your own good:
it's pure gain.

CREON:
                    Old man—all of you! So,
you shoot your arrows at my head like archers at the target—
I even have *him* loosed on me, this fortune-teller.
Oh his ilk has tried to sell me short
and ship me off for years. Well,
drive your bargains, traffic—much as you like—
in the gold of India, silver-gold of Sardis.   1150
You'll never bury that body in the grave,
not even if Zeus's eagles rip the corpse
and wing their rotten pickings off to the throne of god!
Never, not even in fear of such defilement
will I tolerate his burial, that traitor.   1155
Well I know, we can't defile the gods—
no mortal has the power.
                    No,
reverend old Tiresias, all men fall,
it's only human, but the wisest fall obscenely
when they glorify obscene advice with rhetoric—   1160
all for their own gain.

TIRESIAS:
Oh god, is there a man alive
who knows, who actually believes . . .

CREON:
                                   What now?
What earth-shattering truth are you about to utter?

TIRESIAS:
. . . just how much a sense of judgment, wisdom   1165
is the greatest gift we have?

CREON:
                          Just as much, I'd say,
as a twisted mind is the worst affliction known.

TIRESIAS:
You are the one who's sick, Creon, sick to death.

CREON:
I am in no mood to trade insults with a seer.

TIRESIAS:
You have already, calling my prophecies a lie.

CREON:
                                   Why not?   1170
You and the whole breed of seers are mad for money!

TIRESIAS:
And the whole race of tyrants lusts for filthy gain.

CREON:
This slander of yours—
are you aware you're speaking to the king?

TIRESIAS:
Well aware. Who helped you save the city?

CREON:
                                        You—   1175
you have your skills, old seer, but you lust for injustice!

TIRESIAS:
You will drive me to utter the dreadful secret in my heart.

CREON:
Spit it out! Just don't speak it out for profit.

TIRESIAS:
Profit? No, not a bit of profit, not for you.

CREON:
Know full well, you'll never buy off my resolve.   1180

TIRESIAS:
Then know this too, learn this by heart!
The chariot of the sun will not race through
so many circuits more, before you have surrendered
one born of your own loins, your own flesh and blood,
a corpse for corpses given in return, since you have thrust　　　1185
to the world below a child sprung for the world above,
ruthlessly lodged a living soul within the grave—
then you've robbed the gods below the earth,
keeping a dead body here in the bright air,
unburied, unsung, unhallowed by the rites.　　　1190

You, you have no business with the dead,
nor do the gods above—this is violence
you have forced upon the heavens.
And so the avengers, the dark destroyers late
but true to the mark, now lie in wait for you,　　　1195
the Furies sent by the gods and the god of death
to strike you down with the pains that you perfected!

There. Reflect on that, tell me I've been bribed.
The day comes soon, no long test of time, not now,
when the mourning cries for men and women break　　　1200
throughout your halls. Great hatred rises against you—
cities in tumult, all whose mutilated sons
the dogs have graced with burial, or the wild beasts
or a wheeling crow that wings the ungodly stench of carrion
back to each city, each warrior's hearth and home.　　　1205

These arrows for your heart! Since you've raked me
I loose them like an archer in my anger,
arrows deadly true. You'll never escape
their burning, searing force,

Motioning to his escort.

Come, boy, take me home.　　　1210
So he can vent his rage on younger men,
and learn to keep a gentler tongue in his head
and better sense than what he carries now.

Exit to the side.

LEADER:

The old man's gone, my king—
terrible prophecies. Well I know,   1215
since the hair on this old head went gray,
he's never lied to Thebes.

CREON:

I know it myself—I'm shaken, torn.
It's a dreadful thing to yield . . . but resist now?
Lay my pride bare to the blows of ruin?   1220
That's dreadful too.

LEADER:

                    But good advice,
Creon, take it now, you must.

CREON:

What should I do? Tell me . . . I'll obey.

LEADER:

Go! Free the girl from the rocky vault
and raise a mound for the body you exposed.   1225

CREON:

That's your advice? You think I should give in?

LEADER:

Yes, my king, quickly. Disasters sent by the gods
cut short our follies in a flash.

CREON:

                              Oh it's hard,
giving up the heart's desire . . . but I will do it—
no more fighting a losing battle with necessity.   1230

LEADER:

Do it now, go, don't leave it to others.

CREON:

Now—I'm on my way! Come, each of you,
take up axes, make for the high ground,
over there, quickly! I and my better judgment
have come round to this—I shackled her,   1235
I'll set her free myself. I am afraid . . .
it's best to keep the established laws
to the very day we die.

Rushing out, followed by his
entourage. The CHORUS *clusters*
around the altar.

CHORUS:
God of a hundred names!
                    Great Dionysus—
          Son and glory of Semele! Pride of Thebes—   1240
Child of Zeus whose thunder rocks the clouds—
Lord of the famous lands of evening—
King of the Mysteries!
                    King of Eleusis, Demeter's plain
her breasting hills that welcome in the world—
Great Dionysus!
                    Bacchus, living in Thebes   1245
the mother-city of all your frenzied women—
                              Bacchus
     living along the Ismenus' rippling waters
standing over the field sown with the Dragon's teeth!

You—we have seen you through the flaring smoky fires,
     your torches blazing over the twin peaks   1250
where nymphs of the hallowed cave climb onward
                    fired with you, your sacred rage—
we have seen you at Castalia's running spring
and down from the heights of Nysa crowned with ivy
the greening shore rioting vines and grapes   1255
          down you come in your storm of wild women
                    ecstatic, mystic cries—
                              Dionysus—
down to watch and ward the roads of Thebes!

First of all cities, Thebes you honor first
you and your mother, bride of the lightning—   1260
come, Dionysus! now your people lie
in the iron grip of plague,
come in your racing, healing stride
                    down Parnassus' slopes
or across the moaning straits.

                              Lord of the dancing—   1265
dance, dance the constellations breathing fire!
Great master of the voices of the night!
Child of Zeus, God's offspring, come, come forth!
Lord, king, dance with your nymphs, swirling, raving
arm-in-arm in frenzy through the night   1270
    they dance you, Iacchus—
                    Dance, Dionysus
giver of all good things!

                              Enter a MESSENGER *from the side.*

MESSENGER:
                    Neighbors,
friends of the house of Cadmus and the kings,
there's not a thing in this mortal life of ours
I'd praise or blame as settled once for all.
Fortune lifts and Fortune fells the lucky   1275
and unlucky every day. No prophet on earth
can tell a man his fate. Take Creon:
there was a man to rouse your envy once,
as I see it. He saved the realm from enemies,   1280
taking power, he alone, the lord of the fatherland,
he set us true on course—he flourished like a tree
with the noble line of sons he bred and reared . . .
and now it's lost, all gone.

Believe me,
when a man has squandered his true joys,   1285
he's good as dead, I tell you, a living corpse.
Pile up riches in your house, as much as you like—
live like a king with a huge show of pomp,
but if real delight is missing from the lot,
I wouldn't give you a wisp of smoke for it,   1290
not compared with joy.

LEADER:
What now?
What new grief do you bring the house of kings?

MESSENGER:
Dead, dead—and the living are guilty of their death!

LEADER:
Who's the murderer? Who is dead? Tell us.

MESSENGER:
Haemon's gone, his blood spilled by the very hand—   1295

LEADER:
His father's or his own?

MESSENGER:
His own . . .
raging mad with his father for the death—

LEADER:
Oh great seer,
you saw it all, you brought your word to birth!

MESSENGER:
Those are the facts. Deal with them as you will.
As he turns to go, EURYDICE *enters
from the palace.*

LEADER:

Look, Eurydice. Poor woman, Creon's wife,   1300
so close at hand. By chance perhaps,
unless she's heard the news about her son.

EURYDICE:

My countrymen,
all of you—I caught the sound of your words
as I was leaving to do my part,
to appeal to queen Athena with my prayers.   1305
I was just loosing the bolts, opening the doors,
when a voice filled with sorrow, family sorrow,
struck my ears, and I fell back, terrified,
into the women's arms—everything went black.
Tell me the news, again, whatever it is . . .   1310
sorrow and I are hardly strangers.
I can bear the worst.

MESSENGER:

I—dear lady,
I'll speak as an eye-witness. I was there.
And I won't pass over one word of the truth.
Why should I try to soothe you with a story,   1315
only to prove a liar in a moment?
Truth is always best.
So,
I escorted your lord, I guided him
to the edge of the plain where the body lay,
Polynices, torn by the dogs and still unmourned.   1320
And saying a prayer to Hecate of the Crossroads,
Pluto too, to hold their anger and be kind,
we washed the dead in a bath of holy water
and plucking some fresh branches, gathering . . .
what was left of him, we burned them all together   1325
and raised a high mound of native earth, and then
we turned and made for that rocky vault of hers,
the hollow, empty bed of the bride of Death.

And far off, one of us heard a voice,
a long wail rising, echoing   1330
out of that unhallowed wedding-chamber,
he ran to alert the master and Creon pressed on,
closer—the strange, inscrutable cry came sharper,
throbbing around him now, and he let loose
a cry of his own, enough to wrench the heart,   1335
"Oh god, am I the prophet now? going down
the darkest road I've ever gone? My son—
it's *his* dear voice, he greets me! Go, men,
closer, quickly! Go through the gap,
the rocks are dragged back—   1340
right to the tomb's very mouth—and look,
see if it's Haemon's voice I think I hear,
or the gods have robbed me of my senses."

The king was shattered. We took his orders,
went and searched, and there in the deepest,   1345
dark recesses of the tomb we found her . . .
hanged by the neck in a fine linen noose,
strangled in her veils—and the boy,
his arms flung around her waist,
clinging to her, wailing for his bride,   1350
dead and down below, for his father's crimes
and the bed of his marriage blighted by misfortune.
When Creon saw him, he gave a deep sob,
he ran in, shouting, crying out to him,
"Oh my child—what have you done? what seized you,   1355
what insanity? what disaster drove you mad?
Come out, my son! I beg you on my knees!"
But the boy gave him a wild burning glance,
spat in his face, not a word in reply,
he drew his sword—his father rushed out,   1360
running as Haemon lunged and missed!—
and then, doomed, desperate with himself,
suddenly leaning his full weight on the blade,
he buried it in his body, halfway to the hilt.

And still in his senses, pouring his arms around her,　　　1365
he embraced the girl and breathing hard,
released a quick rush of blood,
bright red on her cheek glistening white.
And there he lies, body enfolding body . . .
he has won his bride at last, poor boy,　　　1370
not here but in the houses of the dead.

Creon shows the world that of all the ills
afflicting men the worst is lack of judgment.

> EURYDICE *turns and reenters the*
> *palace.*

LEADER:
What do you make of that? The lady's gone,
without a word, good or bad.

MESSENGER:
　　　　　　　　　　　I'm alarmed too　　　1375
but here's my hope—faced with her son's death
she finds it unbecoming to mourn in public.
Inside, under her roof, she'll set her women
to the task and wail the sorrow of the house.
She's too discreet. She won't do something rash.　　　1380

LEADER:
I'm not so sure. To me, at least,
a long heavy silence promises danger,
just as much as a lot of empty outcries.

MESSENGER:
We'll see if she's holding something back,
hiding some passion in her heart.　　　1385
I'm going in. You may be right—who knows?
Even too much silence has its dangers.

> *Exit to the palace. Enter* CREON
> *from the side, escorted by attendants*
> *carrying* HAEMON's *body on a bier.*

LEADER:

> The king himself! Coming toward us,
> look, holding the boy's head in his hands.
> Clear, damning proof, if it's right to say so—   *1390*
> proof of his own madness, no one else's,
>> no, his own blind wrongs.

CREON:

>>>>>> Ohhh,
> so senseless, so insane . . . my crimes,
> my stubborn, deadly—
> Look at us, the killer, the killed,   *1395*
> father and son, the same blood—the misery!
> My plans, my mad fanatic heart,
> my son, cut off so young!
> Ai, dead, lost to the world,
> not through your stupidity, no, my own.

LEADER:

>>>>>> Too late,   *1400*

too late, you see what justice means.

CREON:

>>>>> Oh I've learned
> through blood and tears! Then, it was then,
> when the god came down and struck me—a great weight
> shattering, driving me down that wild savage path,
> ruining, trampling down my joy. Oh the agony,   *1405*
>> the heartbreaking agonies of our lives.

>>>>> *Enter the* MESSENGER *from the*
>>>>> *palace.*

MESSENGER:

>>>>> Master,
what a hoard of grief you have, and you'll have more.
The grief that lies to hand you've brought yourself—

>>>>> *Pointing to* HAEMON's *body.*

the rest, in the house, you'll see it all too soon.

CREON:
What now? What's worse than this?

MESSENGER:
                              The queen is dead.   1410
The mother of this dead boy . . . mother to the end—
poor thing, her wounds are fresh.

CREON:
                         No, no,
     harbor of Death, so choked, so hard to cleanse!—
     why me? why are you killing me?
     Herald of pain, more words, more grief?   1415
     I died once, you kill me again and again!
     What's the report, boy . . . some news for me?
     My wife dead? O dear god!
     Slaughter heaped on slaughter?
                         The doors open; the body of
                         EURYDICE *is brought out on her bier.*

MESSENGER:
                              See for yourself:
now they bring her body from the palace.

CREON:
                              Oh no,   1420
     another, a second loss to break the heart.
     What next, what fate still waits for me?
     I just held my son in my arms and now,
     look, a new corpse rising before my eyes—
         wretched, helpless mother—O my son!   1425

MESSENGER:
She stabbed herself at the altar,
then her eyes went dark, after she'd raised
a cry for the noble fate of Megareus, the hero
killed in the first assault, then for Haemon,
then with her dying breath she called down   1430
torments on your head—you killed her sons.

CREON:
                              Oh the dread,
    I shudder with dread! Why not kill me too?—
    run me through with a good sharp sword?
    Oh god, the misery, anguish—
    I, I'm churning with it, going under.   1435

MESSENGER:
Yes, and the dead, the woman lying there,
piles the guilt of all their deaths on you.

CREON:
How did she end her life, what bloody stroke?

MESSENGER:
She drove home to the heart with her own hand,
once she learned her son was dead . . . that agony.   1440

CREON:
    And the guilt is all mine—
    can never be fixed on another man,
    no escape for me. I killed you,
    I, god help me, I admit it all!

                    To his attendants.

    Take me away, quickly, out of sight.   1445
    I don't even exist—I'm no one. Nothing.

LEADER:

Good advice, if there's any good in suffering.
Quickest is best when troubles block the way.

CREON:

Kneeling in prayer.

Come, let it come!—that best of fates for me
that brings the final day, best fate of all.   1450
Oh quickly, now—
so I never have to see another sunrise.

LEADER:

That will come when it comes;
we must deal with all that lies before us.
The future rests with the ones who tend the future.   1455

CREON:

That prayer—I poured my heart into that prayer!

LEADER:

No more prayers now. For mortal men
there is no escape from the doom we must endure.

CREON:

Take me away, I beg you, out of sight.
A rash, indiscriminate fool!   1460
I murdered you, my son, against my will—
you too, my wife . . .

                    Wailing wreck of a man,
whom to look to? where to lean for support?

Desperately turning from HAEMON *to*
EURYDICE *on their biers.*

Whatever I touch goes wrong—once more
a crushing fate's come down upon my head!   1465

The MESSENGER *and attendants lead*
CREON *into the palace.*

CHORUS:

>Wisdom is by far the greatest part of joy,
>and reverence toward the gods must be safeguarded.
>The mighty words of the proud are paid in full
>with mighty blows of fate, and at long last
>those blows will teach us wisdom.   1470

The old citizens exit to the side.

NOTES ON THE TRANSLATION

ANTIGONE

4 *The two of us:* the intimate bond between the two sisters (and the two brothers) is emphasized in the original Greek by an untranslatable linguistic usage—the dual, a set of endings for verbs, nouns and adjectives that is used only when two subjects are concerned (there is a different set of endings—the plural—for more than two). Significantly, Antigone no longer uses these forms to speak of herself and her sister after Ismene refuses to help her bury their brother.

6 *Our lives are pain:* the translation here is dictated rather by the logic of the passage than the actual Greek words. The phrase in Greek to which these words correspond is clearly corrupt (it seems to interrupt a culminating series of negatives with a positive), and no satisfactory emendation or explanation has ever been offered.

12 *The doom reserved for enemies:* this seems to refer to the fact that Creon had also exposed the corpses of the other six (non-Theban) attackers of the city; they are foreign "enemies," whereas Polynices, for Antigone, is still a "friend," since he was a blood relative. The exposure of the other bodies was part of the legend as we find it elsewhere (in Euripides' play *The Suppliants,* for example) and is referred to in Tiresias' speech to Creon later in our play (1202–5). Some scholars interpret the Greek differently, to mean "evils planned by enemies," i.e., by Creon.

43 *Stoning to death:* a penalty which involves the community in the execution; it is therefore particularly appropriate in cases of treason, where the criminal has acted against the whole citizen body. It depends, of course, on the willingness of the citizens to carry it out, and it is noticeable that though Creon later refuses to accept Haemon's assertion that public opinion favors Antigone (776–82), he changes his mind about the penalty and substitutes one which does not require citizen participation.

52 *Will you lift up his body . . . ?* If she is to bury the body (and she speaks of "lifting" it), Antigone obviously needs Ismene's help; without it all she can do is perform a symbolic ritual—sprinkling the corpse with dust and pouring libations.

88 *An outrage sacred to the gods:* literally, "committing a holy crime." What is criminal in the eyes of Creon is holy in the eyes of the gods Antigone champions.

113 EXIT ANTIGONE. There is of course no stage direction in our text (see pp. 389–90). We suggest that Antigone leaves the stage here not only because after her speech she obviously has nothing more to say to Ismene, but also because the effect of her harsh dismissal of her sister would be weakened if she then stood silent while Ismene had the last word. We suggest that she starts out toward the side exit and Ismene speaks to her retreating figure before she herself goes off stage, but through the door into the palace.

117–79 The *parodos* (literally, "the way past") is the name of the space between the end of the stage building and the end of the spectators' benches (see Introduction, pp. 19, 258). Through these two passageways the chorus made its entrance, proceeding to the *orchêstra,* the circular dancing-floor in front of the stage building. The word *parodos* is also used to denote the first choral song, the lines which the chorus chants as it marches in.

This song is a victory ode, a celebration of the city's escape from capture, sack and destruction. The chorus imagines the enemy running in panic before the rising sun; their shields are white (122) perhaps because the name Argos suggests the adjective *argos,* which means "shining." The enemy assault of the previous day they compare to an eagle descending on its prey, but it was met and routed by a dragon (138); the Thebans believed that they were descended from dragons' teeth, which, sown in the soil by Cadmus, their first king, turned into armored men. Of all the seven chieftains who attacked the gates, Capaneus was the most violent and boastful; high on a scaling ladder he reached the top of the wall but was struck down by a lightning bolt of Zeus (147). The defeat of the other attackers is the work of Ares (154), the war god, who is also one of the patron deities of Thebes. The seven chieftains were all killed; all seven were stripped of their armor, which was then arranged on wooden frames in the likeness of a warrior. This is what the Greeks called a *tropaion* (our word "trophy"); the Greek word suggests "turning point," and in fact the trophy was set up at the point where the losing side first turned and ran. The god who engineered such reversals was Zeus *Tropaios*— "god of the breaking rout of battle" (159). In the last stanza the dancers address Victory, who is always represented in Greek art as a winged female figure; they look forward to the joys of peace, the revelry associated with the god Dionysus, born of a Theban mother.

188 *Their children:* i.e., the children of Oedipus and Jocasta.

213 *Truer than blood itself:* this is an attempt to bring out in English the double meaning of the word translated "friendships"; the Greek word *philous* means both "friends" and "close relations."

215 *Closely akin:* the Greek word means literally "brother to." But Creon is in fact disregarding the claims of kinship.

278 *Someone's just buried it:* this is a token burial (see n. 52); it is defined in the lines that follow (289–92). The sprinkling of dust and the pouring of a libation were considered the equivalent of burial where nothing more could be done and so were a direct defiance of Creon's order (see 346).

300–1 *Red-hot iron . . . go through fire:* traditional (and hyperbolic) assertions of truthfulness; the reference is to some form of trial by ordeal in which only the liar would get burned.

376–416 The chorus entered the *orchêstra* to the strains of the *parodos;* it now, with the stage area empty of actors, sings the first *stasimon.* The word means something like "stationary"; it distinguishes the songs the chorus sings once it has reached the *orchêstra* (where it will, normally, remain until the end of the play) from the *parodos,* which it sings while marching in. But of course the chorus is not actually stationary; its members dance in formation as they sing.

This famous hymn to the inventiveness and creativeness of man has important thematic significance for the play, in which a ruler, in the name of man's creation, the state, defies age-old laws: the ode ends with a warning that man's energy and resourcefulness may lead him to destruction as well as greatness. But choral odes, though one of their important functions is to suggest and discuss the wider implications of the action, usually have an immediate dramatic relevance as well. In this case the chorus must be thinking of the daring and ingenuity of the person who gave Polynices' body symbolic burial. This does not mean that they are expressing approval of the action; the wonders of the world, of which man is the foremost, are "terrible wonders."

The ode's vision of human history as progress from helplessness to near mastery of the environment reappears in other fifth-century dramatic texts, notably in the *Prometheus Bound* and the Euripidean *Suppliants*. It is likely that all these accounts are based on a book (now lost) by the sophist Protagoras called *The State of Things in the Beginning.*

385 *The breed of stallions:* mules, then, as now, the work animal of a Greek farm.

409 *Weaves in:* this is a literal translation of the reading found in all the manuscripts, *pareirôn.* Though the word occurs elsewhere in fifth-century tragedy, editors have thought the metaphor too violent here; most editors take it as a copyist's mistake for *gerairôn,* which would give the meaning "honors," "reveres."

424 *Act of mad defiance:* the chorus here and later (677, "fury at the heart") can explain Antigone's defiance of power only as mental aberration; Creon speaks in similar terms of the two sisters when Ismene wishes to join her sister in death ("They're both mad, I tell you . . ." 632).

480 *Three . . . libations:* drink-offerings to the dead; they might be of honey, wine, olive oil, or water.

590 The verbs used in this famous line, *synechthein* and *symphilein,* appear nowhere else in Greek literature and may have been expressly coined by Sophocles to express the distinction Antigone is making: that she is incapable of taking sides in her brothers' political hatred for each other but shares in the blood relationship which, she believes, unites them in love in the world below.

645–49 ISMENE. *Dearest Haemon . . .* All the manuscripts give this line to Ismene. But manuscript attributions are very often wrong (see pp. 389–90) and many editors give the line to Antigone. (The phrase in Creon's line that follows, translated "your talk of marriage," could equally well mean "your marriage" and so refer to Antigone, who has not been talking about marriage, instead of Ismene, who has.) If the line is Ismene's, however, Sophocles has given us an Antigone who never mentions Haemon, though we learn later that he loves her more than his own life. But there is a technical reason (apart from any question of interpretation) against giving the line to Antigone: Ismene must have the next reply to Creon (647, "Creon—you're really going to rob your son of Antigone?"), and this would present us with a phenomenon for which we have no parallel—a long exchange of single lines between two actors interrupted for one line by a third. Dawe has recently proposed a solution to this difficulty: to give all three lines (including line 649, the one here assigned to the leader) to Antigone. This is linguistically unassailable (line 647 would then mean: "Creon—you're really going to rob your son of *me?*"); her next line would mean: "It's decided then? I'm going to die?"; and Creon's reply would mean: "Decided, yes. By you and me." This reading has its very attractive aspects but gives us an Antigone whose second line sounds a completely uncharacteristic note of self-pity and is in effect a plea for her life—also uncharacteristic. We have assigned 645 and 647 to Ismene, 649 to the leader of the chorus.

656–700 The chorus sees an explanation for the death which now threatens the two last remaining members of the house of Oedipus: it is the working of a hereditary doom. The reason for it is not given (though legends known to some of the audience traced it back to the wrongdoing of Laius, father of Oedipus) but it is thought of as the work of the gods. In the opening speech of the play Antigone spoke in similar terms and attributed the sorrows of her line to Zeus. And in the second unit of this *stasimon* the chorus sings of the power of Zeus and man's inability to override it. So far, clearly, they have been meditating on the fate of Antigone, but their reflections proceed along a line which does not seem relevant to her case. The law of Zeus is that

> no towering form of greatness
>> enters into the lives of mortals
>>> free and clear of ruin. (687–89)

As they develop this theme along lines thoroughly familiar to the audience, which shared this instinctive feeling that greatness is dangerous, it must have become clear that their words express anxiety not for Antigone, the helpless and condemned, but for Creon, the man who holds and wields supreme power in the state.

667–69 *Sorrows of the house . . . piling on the sorrows of the dead.* This
could be read as "sorrows of the dead . . . fall on the sorrows of the
living." Both interpretations come to much the same thing.

676 *Bloody knife: kopis* is the Greek word. The manuscripts all read *ko-
nis,* which means "dust." It is true that the dust she has thrown on
Polynices' corpse has brought her to her death, but the metaphor
seems too violent and most editors print *kopis,* a conjecture made by
Jortin, an English scholar of the eighteenth century.

711–12 *Than you, / whatever good direction . . .* The Greek is ambiguous
and could mean "than your good leadership" or "than you, if you
give proper leadership."

736 *Zeus . . . kindred blood:* Zeus *Homaimos* (see Glossary).

794 *Spread them . . . empty.* A metaphor from writing tablets, two slats of
wood covered with wax, on which the message was inscribed. It
would be delivered closed and sealed; the recipient would open it and
read—in this case to find the tablet blank.

872–73 *Short rations . . . piety demands . . .* The city would be kept "free
of defilement" not only because (contrary to Creon's first decision)
the citizens would not be involved in stoning Antigone to death but
also because, if Antigone were to starve to death (or commit suicide),
there would literally be no blood on anyone's hands. Greek supersti-
tious belief thought of responsibility for killing in terms of pollution
by the blood of the victim, which called for blood in return. We
know of no parallels to Creon's sentence, except the similar punishment inflicted in Rome on Vestal Virgins who broke their vows of
chastity.

879–94 *Love . . .* The Greek world *erôs* has a narrower field of meaning
than its English equivalent; it denotes the passionate aspect of sexual
attraction, an irresistible force which brings its victims close to madness.
The immediate occasion of this hymn to Eros is of course the chorus' fear that Haemon, infuriated by the prospect of losing Antigone,
may "do something violent" (862). But the song also reminds the audience that Creon has now offended not only the gods who preside
over the lower world and those who sustain the bonds of family
friendship, but also Eros and Aphrodite who, as the concluding lines
of the ode emphasize, are great powers in the universe—"Throned in
power, side-by-side with the mighty laws!" (892).

889 *This kindred strife:* the Greek adjective *xynaimon* (literally, "common-blood") recalls Haemon's name.

895–969 The first half of the scene which follows the choral ode is a lyric dialogue known as a *kommos:* actor and chorus sing in responsion. At first the chorus addresses Antigone in a march-type rhythm (anapests) that was probably chanted rather than sung; she replies in song, in fully lyric meters. At line 943, as emotion rises to a high pitch, the chorus, too, breaks into full song. Creon's harsh intervention (969) is couched in iambic spoken verse, and Antigone uses the same medium for her farewell speech (978–1021). But the scene ends in the chanted rhythm of marching anapests as Antigone is led off to her tomb (1027–34).

909 *Not crowned with glory . . .* The usual version of this line is: "crowned with glory . . ." The Greek word *oukoun* can be negative or positive, depending on the accent, which determines the pronunciation: since these written accents were not yet in use in Sophocles' time, no one will ever know for sure which meaning he intended. We take the view that the chorus is expressing pity for Antigone's ignominious and abnormal death; she has no funeral at which her fame and praise are recited, she will not die by either of the usual causes—violence or disease—but by a living death. It is, as they say, her own choice; she is "a law to [herself]" (912).

915 *Niobe* boasted that her children were more beautiful than Apollo and Artemis, the children of Leto by Zeus. Apollo and Artemis killed Niobe's twelve (or fourteen) children with bow and arrow; Niobe herself, inconsolably weeping, turned to stone. On Mount Sipylus, in Asia Minor, there was a cliff face which from a distance looked like a weeping woman; it was identified with Niobe.

925 *But she was a god . . .* The chorus reproves Antigone for comparing her own death to that of Niobe, who was not strictly a god, but moved on terms of equality with the gods. The chorus' condescending tone accounts for Antigone's indignant outburst in the next few lines.

944 *Smashing against the high throne of Justice!* The text is very disturbed here. Different readings would add the detail "with your foot" (or "feet") and a radically different sense: "falling in supplication before the high throne . . ."

957 *Your marriage murders mine:* Polynices had married the daughter of Adrastus of Argos, to seal the alliance which enabled him to march against Thebes.

977 The Greek word translated "stranger's rights," *metoikias,* had a precise technical sense in Athens; it described the status of a resident alien who was not a full citizen. Creon speaks as if Antigone had already forfeited her citizenship by her action and become a *metoikos,* a resident alien; he will now deprive her of even that status, by burying her alive. Similarly at lines 940 and 956 Antigone speaks of herself as an alien, *metoikos,* both in the world of the living and that of the dead.

988 *My loving brother, Eteocles . . .* The name Eteocles does not appear in the Greek but has been added by the translator to remove a possible ambiguity.

989 *When you died . . .* Antigone's speech has been judged adversely by many critics, who suspect its authenticity; some would go so far as to suppress the whole passage from this point on; others content themselves with removing lines 993 to 1012 (904–5 through 920 in the Greek). We believe the whole of the speech is genuine; for a defense of this position, see the Introduction, pp. 45–50.

1028 *First gods of the race:* the Theban royal house was descended from Cadmus, whose wife Harmonia was the daughter of Aphrodite and Ares. Dionysus was the son of Zeus and Semele, a daughter of Cadmus. See the Genealogy, p. 425.

1035–90 *Danaë, Danaë . . .* The dramatic relevance of the mythological material exploited in this choral ode is not as clear to us as it must have been to the original audience; the second half of the ode, in particular, alludes to stories of which we have only fragmentary, late and conflicting accounts.

The chorus, which reprimanded Antigone for comparing herself to Niobe, now tries to find some satisfactory parallels. Acrisius, king of Argos, was told by an oracle that his grandson would be the cause of his death. He had only one child, Danaë, and, to prevent her from bearing a child, he shut her up in a bronze prison (a tower in some accounts, or, as here, a sort of underground vault). But Zeus, in the form of golden sunlight, reached her and she gave birth to the hero Perseus, who, many years later, after killing the Gorgon Medusa and rescuing the princess Andromeda from the sea monster, accidentally killed his grandfather Acrisius at an athletic contest. The point of comparison with Antigone is clearly the imprisonment in an underground room, and the fact that the room was for Danaë a place to which a forbidden bridegroom forced an entrance will not be lost on the audience when, later on, it hears of Haemon's entry into the tomb of Antigone, and its tragic sequel. But, the parallel once established, the chorus goes on to sing of the power of fate, which no human power (wealth, military strength, fortifications, fleets—the powers of the state) can defy. Acrisius could not escape what was predicted; but what has this to do with Antigone? The resources of power are Creon's, not hers, and he, like Acrisius, tried to prevent the consummation of a marriage. In these lines the chorus is made to express, even if it may not, as a character, understand fully the implication of its own words, its fear for Creon, the beginning of its disenchantment with his course of action.

The next parallel with Antigone, Lycurgus, king of the barbarous Thracians, also has imprisonment as its base. Lycurgus (like Pentheus in Euripides' *Bacchae*) attempted to suppress the worship of Dionysus; he pursued the wild women devotees on the hills, laid hands on the god, mocked and insulted him. Dionysus confined him in a rock—a rocky cave or a miraculous stone envelope—and he went mad. (In one version of the legend, not hinted at here but probably known to the audience, he killed his son in his mad fit.) Here imprisonment, the connection with Antigone, is overshadowed by the ominous resemblances to Creon: he is the one who uses force against a woman, against the gods of the underworld; his is the angry, taunting voice, the frenzied rage. And he will be responsible in the end for the death of his son.

For the last two stanzas of the ode there is no sure line of interpretation. The myth to which it refers (but so cryptically that only two of the people involved are named in the text) told the story of Cleopatra, daughter of an Athenian princess and Boreas, the North Wind. She was married to the Thracian king Phineus, by whom she had two sons. They were blinded by Phineus' second wife; in some versions Cleopatra was already dead, in others she was imprisoned by the new wife and later released. (In some versions, the sons were imprisoned too—like Antigone, in a tomb.) Sophocles could rely on the audience's familiarity with this material (he wrote two plays dealing with Phineus) but we are left to grasp at straws. The last lines of the ode, an address to Antigone which echoes the chorus' similar address at the beginning ("my child," 1042 and 1090) suggests strongly that Antigone is compared to Cleopatra here, as she is to Danaë in the opening lines. In that case Sophocles is almost certainly referring to a version (perhaps that of one of his own plays) in which Cleopatra, like Danaë and Antigone, was imprisoned. We have therefore taken the liberty, in order to produce a translation which makes some kind of sense, of putting this crucial detail into the text. But the reader is warned that lines 1080–1081—"their mother doomed to chains, / walled off in a tomb of stone"—have no equivalent in the Greek text.

1096 *Never wavered from your advice before:* this may be just an acknowl-edgment of the omnipresence of Tiresias in Theban affairs over many generations. On the other hand it may refer to a legend that Tiresias advised Creon, during the attack by the Seven, that Thebes could only be saved by the sacrifice of his son Megareus (who did in fact give his life for his fellow-citizens). Anyone in the audience who re-membered this might see bitter irony in Creon's line (1098) "I owe you a great deal, I swear to that." The death of Megareus will later (1428–31) be blamed on Creon by his wife Eurydice.

1102 *Warnings of my craft:* in this speech Tiresias describes the results of two different techniques of foretelling the future: interpretation, first, of the movements and voices of birds; next, of the behavior of the animal flesh burnt in sacrifice to the gods. The birds, as Tiresias tells us later (1125–26), have been eating the flesh of the corpse exposed by Creon's order; their voices, normally intelligible to the prophet, now convey nothing but their fury as they fight each other. Tiresias turns to the other method of divination, but the fire will not blaze up; it is quenched by the abnormal ooze from the long thighbones. These are all signs that the gods are "deaf to our prayers," as the prophet soon tells Creon (1127).

1150 *Silver-gold of Sardis:* electrum, a natural mixture of silver and gold ("white gold") found in the river near Sardis in Asia Minor.

1192–93 *Violence / you have forced upon the heavens:* by leaving a corpse exposed Creon has not only deprived the lower gods of their rights, he has also polluted with death the province of the Olympian gods of the upper air. The Furies, avenging spirits of both lower and upper gods, lie in wait for him now.

1200 *Cries for men and women break / throughout your halls:* Tiresias prophesies the deaths of Haemon and Eurydice.

1201–2 *Great hatred . . . cities in tumult:* Creon was eventually forced to bury the bodies of the other champions, so Athenian legend ran, by an Athenian army under the leadership of Theseus (this is the theme of Euripides' *Suppliants*). But in the next generation, the sons of the Seven, the *Epigonoi,* attacked Thebes again and this time succeeded in taking the city.

1239–72 *God of a hundred names! . . .* The tone of this choral song is one of exultation; the old men rejoice that Creon has seen the error of his ways and call on the Theban god Dionysus to appear, to come dancing, and as a healer to lead the joyous celebration. The hopes expressed in the song are quickly belied by the tragic events announced by the messenger; a similar ironic sequence is to be found in *Oedipus the King* (1195–1310). The hymn to Dionysus is constructed along the lines of real religious hymns: first the invocation of the god under his (or her) many titles, then a reference to the god's place of origin (Thebes), an enumeration of the most important places of his worship (Delphi, Nysa), an appeal to the god to come to the aid of the worshiper, and finally an invocation of the god by new names and titles.

1243 *King of Eleusis:* Iacchus (1271), the young god associated with Demeter and Persephone in the mystery religion centered at Eleusis in Attica, was often identified with Dionysus (*Bakchos*). Dionysus was supposed to be present, in the winter season, at Apollo's site, Delphi on Mount Parnassus, where the "twin peaks" of the cliffs (1250) towered above the sanctuary and the Castalian spring flowed below (1253). *Nysa* (1254) is a name given to many mountains in the ancient world, but the reference here is probably to the one on the long island of Euboea, opposite Theban territory, and separated from it by the Euripus ("the moaning straits," 1265).

1321 *Hecate of the Crossroads:* a goddess associated with burial grounds and the darkness of the night; offerings to her were left at crossroads. Here she is thought of as associated with Pluto (another name of Hades), as one whose privileges have been curtailed by Creon's action.

1341 *The tomb's very mouth:* Sophocles evidently imagined Antigone's prison on the model of the great domed Mycenaean tombs, built of stone and then covered with earth. Haemon has prised loose some of the stones to effect an entrance; once inside this, Creon's men go along a passage to the "mouth" (i.e., the doorway) of the main chamber.

1346–47 *We found her . . . / hanged by the neck . . .* The details are not clear. These words seem to mean that the speaker saw Antigone still hanging. At the end of his speech he describes Haemon as embracing Antigone—"there he lies, body enfolding body" (1369)—in terms which clearly imply that her body has been lowered to the ground. Sophocles does not tell us how or when this happened, but we probably are meant to imagine that Haemon cut the rope with his sword—which would be the normal, instinctive reaction to the sight of a hanging body.